Becoming Japanese

the world of the
pre-school
child

Becoming Japanese

the world of the
pre-school
child

Joy Hendry

University of Hawaii Press
Honolulu

Published in North America by
University of Hawaii Press
2840 Kolowalu Street
Honolulu, Hawaii 96822

Paperback edition published in 1989, reprinted 1992

Simultaneously published in Great Britain by
Manchester University Press,
Oxford Road, Manchester M13 9PL, UK

Library of Congress cataloging in publication data

Hendry, Joy.
   Becoming Japanese.
   Bibliography: p. 182
   Includes index.
   1. Child rearing – Japan – Case studies. 2. Parent
and child – Japan – Case studies. 3. Socialization – Case
studies. I. Title.
HQ792.J3H46   1986   305.2′33′0952   86-19154
ISBN 0–8248–1092–9

ISBN 0–8248–1215–8 (Pbk.)

Photoset in Linotron Sabon with Syntax
by Northern Phototypesetting Co., Bolton
Printed in Great Britain
by Bell and Bain Ltd., Glasgow

Contents

Illustrations 1–15 appear between pages 70 and 71

Introduction

A cluster of little Japanese children at play some-
how suggests to me a grand picture gallery, a picture gallery of a nation . . . Each little picture . . . is
perfect in itself; yet on closer study it will be found
that the children are more than mere pictures.
They tell us the truths of Japan.[1]

This perhaps rather casual comment, accompanying the artistic
impressions of a Western visitor to Japan at the end of the nineteenth
century, leads aptly into the subject matter of this book. The
apparent charm small Japanese children hold for foreign visitors has
occasioned casual comment from many writers, often those seriously
interested in quite different topics.[2] The word which most often
recurs in their writings is indulgence. It is commented that the
children are greatly loved and fussed over, rarely punished. There
have been only a few attempts to look more deeply into the child
rearing practices,[3] but as the nineteenth-century travellers suggest,
closer inspection reveals that this is a rich and fruitful area for
gaining an insight into some 'truths of Japan'. For, despite the
apparent indulgence, adults in Japan take very seriously the matter
of child care, and the training of children for their future roles begins
very early in their lives. This book is concerned with the quite
conscious efforts adults make to prepare children for the social
world into which they will grow.

A child in any society learns to perceive the world through language, spoken and unspoken, through ritual enacted, indeed,
through the total symbolic system which structures and constrains
that world. Thus, the essentially biological being gradually becomes

a member of society sharing a system of classification with other members, with whom he or she thus learns to communicate and interact in a meaningful way. This process is part of socialisation. Since much social learning takes place in the first few years of life, which are not easy to recall as one grows beyond them, many socially relative categories are perceived as quite natural and normal. Thus, for an outsider trying to make sense of another society, such basic differences may not easily come to the surface. Indeed, the Japanese–American anthropologist Harumi Befu has recently attributed what he sees as a persistence on the part of Westerners to interpret Japanese society in terms of a 'partial model' to the fact that foreign academics have 'not been socialized from infancy to develop tentacles sensitive to cultural cues which are essential for evaluating cultural propositions (e.g. meaning) at the gut level.'[4]

While we, as Westerners, evidently cannot rectify this deficiency entirely – nor indeed would it be considered advantageous by all to lose the outsider's view – it seems likely that a study of adults' interactions with small children could in any society add an important perspective to an understanding of its fundamental principles. It was with such an aim in view that the research for this book was conducted. Indeed, it was initially planned for rather personal reasons. My own children were at this early stage of development, and, as a social anthropologist of Japan, it seemed an excellent way to combine my professional interests with the maternal curiosity aroused by my own circumstances. It was only when we were well established in the field that it became clear how much emphasis is placed on early training in the Japanese case, and what a rich mine of information about Japanese society I had unearthed.

The focus is on the pre-school period, which, as it turns out, is regarded by most Japanese as a vitally important time of preparation for later development. Thus, men as well as the women more directly involved, will launch into long speeches about the topic at a theoretical level, and innumerable books and pamphlets are published by a variety of prestigious people to help mothers and other caretakers in practice. So different are Japanese attitudes to small children from the old English adage that children should be 'seen and not heard' that the first chapter of this book is devoted to a detailed exposition of Japanese collective ideas as they are expressed in various ways.

Of course, there has been considerable exchange of ideas on the subject of early-childhood education between different cultures. Many Western practices have been tried and adopted in Japan; some have been rejected; similarly some traditional Japanese customs seem to have become popular in Western countries though they may not have come directly from that nation in particular. Thus, for example, while Japanese introduce prams and push-chairs to their children, parents in the West have started carrying their children in close physical contact; and the 'family bed' which has been the subject of much discussion in the West, has its well-accepted form in Japan.[5] Nevertheless, while our child psychologists argue amongst themselves about even the importance of the early period,[6] and change their views in time for almost every new sibling born into a family, there seems to be a remarkable consistency in the advice of Japanese experts. Thus, the same principles which are enunciated in the manuals underlie the frequent television programmes, both those for small children to watch, and those to aid the adults dealing with them. This has the additional advantage for the observer of making possible a degree of generalisation from research carried out in quite a limited number of families.

The longest period of investigation in fact took place in Tateyama City in Chiba prefecture during six months in 1981. Visits were also made to Tokyo, where I had some long-established informants, and a month was spent in a rural area of Fukuoka prefecture in a village called Kurotsuchi where I had previously carried out a year's intensive research. The most revealing material was obtained during informal contact with mothers and other caretakers in what is usually described as participant observation. My older son attended a kindergarten in Tateyama which made me a bona fide member of the PTA and an expected participant in all activities involving parents. We were lent accommodation attached to the kindergarten during our stay in Tateyama, and our nanny taught a few hours a week of English there, which gave us good informal contact with the staff and pupils. My younger son was registered with the local health authorities so that we received the usual attentions afforded pre-school children. Many afternoons were spent in the company of other mothers with small children, some in the neighbourhood, some in the kindergarten network, and one, in particular, a friend of such

3

long-standing that formalities could be dispensed with almost entirely.

After a couple of months of fairly informal discussions with other mothers, I drew up a questionnaire about child-rearing in order to be more systematic in my collection of information. These questions were asked, still in an informal way so as to leave open the possibility of raising new ideas, of some fifty mothers of various educational backgrounds, living in a variety of socio-economic circumstances. Some devoted themselves full-time to their families, some worked outside the home; some lived with their husbands and children only, some were part of extended families; some were in an urban environment, others lived in quite rural areas. Slightly less than half were in Kyushu, mostly in the village of Kurotsuchi, a few were in Tokyo, and the remainder were in and around Tateyama. Further details about the questions and the families are to be found in the Appendix.

This information has been provided to give the reader an idea of the range of families who were involved in the investigation, although many other sources were used. It is possible, however, that the view presented here is biased in favour of certain social groups within Japan. An anthropological investigation, which concentrates on intensive relations with a smallish number of informants, rather than surveys which cover larger numbers of people, cannot easily be representative. However, one of the ideas is to uncover assumptions which underlie the activities of members of a society, and although these may vary from one socio-economic group to another, certain assumptions would seem to be shared, like the language, throughout Japan. It is particularly these which I have tried to present, but that is not to say that there may not be individuals or groups which see things differently.

For most children, the pre-school period involves attendance at a kindergarten or day nursery for a couple of years or more. The two types of institution are similar except that the day nursery, which is designed to cater for the children of working mothers, has longer hours and accepts children from an earlier age than the kindergarten. Considerable time was thus also spent visiting a number of such establishments where, despite various ideological allegiances, it was possible to discern common characteristics, again allowing a degree of generalisation about the principles involved in becoming

Japanese. My presence could hardly pass unnoticed, but I asked the teachers to continue their activities as far as possible in the usual way, and, especially where I was able to spend several sessions in them, I think I was able to observe fairly normal procedure. It was also possible in some cases to study detailed forms filled out by parents about their own children, and these provided a good deal of valuable information.

The middle chapters of this book are concerned with the substance of child-rearing as observed in these various contexts and as discussed by the adults involved. Chapter II presents an overview of the period, with a consideration of the relative importance of different arenas and agents at different stages. Chapter III is concerned with the aims and aspirations of these agents and begins to indicate some of the important values which underlie them. Chapter IV discusses the techniques used to achieve these aims, concentrating particularly on the first arenas of the home and neighbourhood, and drawing for comparative purposes on the comments of other writers on the subject. Chapter V turns from the informal to the formal introduction of a child to its social world and reports on various aspects of life in the kindergartens and day nurseries.

Certain basic principles begin to emerge as important throughout these chapters, and the last part of the book brings these together in an attempt to present some fundamental elements of Japanese society which underlie the training of children to enter a social world. Subjects covered here include the way in which space and time are divided up, the way people are classified, and indeed the way the child learns to see itself within the wider world to which it belongs. Ultimately, the aim is to make it possible for the reader to begin to see the world as a Japanese person might. There are of course many years of further socialisation between the period under discussion and the attainment of adulthood, but I think that it is during this early period that, at least in the Japanese case, many of the most fundamental aspects of society are being passed on.

This approach may seem suggestive of the culture-personality school and its attempts to relate national character and adult personality to child rearing practices. However, I have no training in psychology, or even psychological anthropology, and my aims are limited to a consideration of social factors. Nevertheless, such studies carried out in Japan[7] have by no means been ignored here. In particular, the study in Japanese by Hiroko Hara and Hiroshi Wagatsuma has provided much valuable stimulation, as has the classic study of Ruth Benedict, *The Chrysanthemum and the Sword*. I must also confess a debt to Aberle in the ordering of the material in the middle chapters of this book.[8] Nevertheless, it should be clear from the conclusions that the results may be rather different.

Indeed, it is hoped that as well as providing a revealing new window on Japanese society, this study will also form a contribution to the field of socialisation within the subject of social anthropology. As several writers have pointed out, this is an area of the subject which has been neglected in recent years.[9] Even the Association of Social Anthropologists' volume on the subject, which appeared in 1970, focused on the socialisation of adults and youth, rather than on child training, possibly because of the strong association of the latter with the culture-personality school, which has never been highly regarded in this country. Here I would hope to echo the spirit expressed in the introduction to that volume, 'that it is possible to study socialisation by regular social anthropological means, without special recourse to psychology . . . and . . . it is also possible to draw in psychological concepts, where desired, without necessarily distorting anthropological explanation'.[10]

There is, of course, considerable discussion about what is meant by the term 'socialisation'. Some Americans follow Mead and insist that it must be distinguished from 'enculturation' in the case of a particular society, but there are different views on this.[11] For Mayer, 'socialisation may be broadly defined as the inculcation of skills and attitudes necessary for playing given social roles'.[12] This is close to Aberle's definition,[13] which is cited with several others by Clausen in his introduction to a collection of papers on the subject.[14] 'Most simply', writes Clausen, 'the study of socialisation focusses upon the development of the individual as a social being and participant in society.' This emphasises the recipient's role, while the definitions of Mayer and Aberle emphasise those of the agents concerned. In this book I am mostly concerned with the conscious efforts of adults to bring up their children to be acceptable members of society, and I discuss the indigenous concept involved in some detail in Chapter I.

However, the final chapter turns to the view of the recipients of this activity and thus comes closer to Clausen's view, later elaborated to include 'patterns of social learning, transmitted through child care and training, the acquisition of language and of selfhood, and the learning of social rules and moral norms'.[15] Ultimately, the concern here is with the system of classification which is being passed on, the social categories into which the world in Japan is divided and by which social life is therefore constrained.

This book covers only the pre-school years so it is by no means complete, but is is my contention that, at least in the Japanese case, it is during that time that the foundations are laid for most of the important distinctions which will be carried through to adult life. In view of the quantities of literature available on Japanese society, it would seem to be invidious to try to put this study in a complete social context by including a chapter on Japan, as such a study carried out in a less well-documented society might. It would be necessary greatly to oversimplify things and such a chapter would anyway lay itself open to the temptation to draw only on ideas which fit in with the child-rearing material. It is therefore left to the reader to make comparisons with his or her own knowledge about Japanese society, and partly for this reason I have allowed my theoretical analysis to emerge out of the ethnographic detail, rather than the reverse.

There is no similar work available, and it is hoped that this book will make a valuable contribution to the Western understanding of a nation with whom we are increasingly in contact. Children may seem a far cry from big business and international relations, but an understanding of the most basic assumptions being made by one's counterparts cannot but help understanding at any level, and I feel sure that anyone with an interest in Japan could learn from this book.

I am greatly indebted to the Japan Foundation for supporting the fieldwork for this study, also to the Japanese Ministry of Education, Culture and Science, the Ministry of Welfare, and the municipal authorities in Tateyama and Yame for providing information. I must also thank Mrs Takahashi of Shirayuri Kindergarten for providing our accommodation and help in many other ways there, and my assistant, Takako Shimagami, for arranging our situation in the first place, supporting my work throughout our stay, and acting as an excellent informant. Many other parents, grandparents, teachers and children have contributed in incalculable ways to the research, and my debt is no less great if they are too numerous to mention individually. For accommodation in Kyushu, I must single out the Kumagae and Baba families, who apparently happily and willingly put up with what must have been an extraordinary invasion of their domestic lives, since a researcher with a family in tow must inevitably represent a good deal more trouble than a single individual.

Since our return, I have had the opportunity to try out my ideas and analysis on a number of native Japanese, of whom Mrs Atsuko Shimada and Mrs Nobuko Morimoto have been particularly generous in time, thought and careful comment. I would also like to thank Laura Inoue and Opal Dunn for reading and commenting on a draft of the book. For academic discussion, I am especially indebted to James McMullen, Helen Calloway, Roger Goodman, Peter Riviere, Robert J. Smith and Teigo Yoshida, and, more generally, to the audiences of seminars and conferences at which I have presented parts of this work in the form of papers. The British Academy and the research fund at the Oxford Polytechnic made possible visits to two such conferences. Finally, I must thank my husband for putting up with the extended absence of his family for the period of research, and all sorts of upheaval and interference in his own life occasioned by the project more generally. I hope that my children, who had absolutely no choice in the matter, have not suffered too greatly from the inevitable irregularities which have arisen in their own early development. In an optimistic mood, which would probably not be encouraged by my Japanese counterparts, I believe that they may even have benefited from the experience!

Notes

---

1   Menpes 1901: 137.
2   E.g. Dore 1978: 172; Singer 1973: 31; Benedict 1972: 178; Lanham 1966: 322; Smith 1962: 192; Thunberg quoted in Moloney 1962: 216; Menpes 1901: 147.

3 An exception to this is the detailed study made by Maretzki T. and Maretzki H. 1963. Apart from the sources quoted above, other writers who have considered early child rearing in Japan include Befu 1971: chapter 6, where the topic is discussed, Lebra T. S. 1976: chapter 8 – both of which summarise much of the relevant material from other sources – Norbeck E. & M. 1956 and Vogel E. & S. 1961: 161–6.

4 Befu 1980: 42.

5 The Japanese press has begun to comment on this phenomenon: see, for example, *Asahi Evening News* 27 and 29 May 1982. It has also been noted by Shigaki 1983: 21.

6 See, for example, Elkind 1979: 101.

7 A summary of such works up to 1972 is to be found in Norbeck & Devos 1972, who point out that much of the work was carried out by native Japanese as well as by foreigners. More recently, but in the Japanese language, Hara Hiroko and Wagatsuma Hiroshi have discussed much of the work in *Shitsuke (Child Training)* 1974. A collection of relevant articles was published in 1962 by Bernard Silberman, who also included criticism by Kerlinger (400–13). A more recent criticism by Richard Minear appeared in the *Japan Interpreter* 1980: 36–59.

8 Aberle 1961: 389–91.

9 For example, Mayer 1970: xiv, Richards in Mayer 1970: 7, Hubert 1974: 37, and Middleton 1970: xvi, who is talking in particular about studies of systems of education in their social context.

10 Mayer 1970: xvi.

11 E.g. Williams 1972: 1; Leis 1963: 4–5.

12 Mayer 1970: xiii.

13 1961: 387.

14 1968: 3–4.

15 Clausen 1968: 4.

Chapter One

Japanese views of children

Collective ideas about small children and the amount of attention they should receive vary widely from one society to another. Methods used in bringing up children depend to no small extent on these ideas, and some Japanese views will therefore be presented here to provide a framework for the more detailed material which follows. There is, of course, considerable variation in attitudes within a complex society such as Japan, and views have changed in recent years there as they have in Western societies. There has also been considerable influence from the West into Japan, although this has by no means been indiscriminate. It is quite revealing to examine some of the Western customs which have been rejected in Japan.

What follows, then, includes an analysis of some Japanese concepts associated with child rearing, to demonstrate some of the linguistic constraints which are operating in the Japanese case; some collective ideas about the place of children in Japanese society, and some expectations with regard to their treatment. There is also a section about public concern for small children, and another devoted to the ritual and ceremony carried out during the early period, and some of the symbolic significance of this.

In some parts the description will resemble that which could be made of other societies, and this is no attempt to discuss only that which is uniquely Japanese. As a British observer, my own view is also bound to be different from that of an anthropologist from another Asian country, or even from another Western country, and this bias may well be evident. Nevertheless, the purpose of this chapter is to orient any reader to assumptions and expectations likely to be made by a Japanese person with regard to child-rearing, whether or not they would be shared by the reader, and to provide a context for the chapters which follow.

Some collective ideas

Shitsuke

The Japanese word applied to discussions about child-rearing and early training is *shitsuke* and an analysis of the meanings and associations of this word is quite revealing of general attitudes towards such activity. The standard English translations of the word include 'breeding', 'upbringing', 'training' and 'discipline', but the examples of usage in a popular Japanese–English dictionary are indicative of the significance of the concept. These are phrases which translate into English as 'The boy became depraved from lack of family training', 'Children are plastic in the hands of parents', and 'Home instruction is of the first importance in nurture of a child'.[1]

Definitions in Japanese dictionaries include the idea of the inculcation of good manners in a child, the passing on of daily customs, and the teaching of correct behaviour. The word is usually written in phonetic script, but there is a Chinese character, which was in fact invented by the Japanese to apply to this concept. It is (躾), made up of two parts, (身) and (美), which have the meanings of 'body' and 'beauty' respectively, which may legitimately give the word an earlier meaning of 'to beautify the body'. Japanese commentators discussing the word quote the folklorist Kunio Yanagita's assessment that this character came into use for samurai houses from the Muromachi period (1392–1568), but that its more modern meaning is also concerned with educational direction.[2] The idea is significant, however, for it underlies the very approach of Japanese to child training. In a literal translation of a widely used definition of *shitsuke*, from a dictionary of folklore, the meaning is said to be 'the putting into the body of a child the arts of living and good manners in order to create one grown-up person', (literally, one portion of a social person – *ichininmae no shakaijin*).[3] Another such definition, quoted by Hara and Wagatsuma, is similar: 'the putting into the body of a child the patterns of living, ways of conduct of daily life and a mastery of manners and correct behaviour'.[4]

Western commentators have noted that 'etiquette' is one of the objects of overriding concern in the training of small children,[5] which implies a 'beautifying of the body' even in English, but there is something more involved in the Japanese concept. On a television programme during which the character for *shitsuke* was discussed, it was pointed out that the 'body' part of the character may also be pronounced *shin*, which is homophonous with 'heart', although this should be written differently (心), so that the meaning would then be that the body, including the heart, were being beautified in the process of child training. Indeed, the first on the list of objectives prescribed for kindergartens in the Japanese 1947 School Education Law (Article 78) includes the phrase 'to effect a harmonious development of bodily functions',[6] and the 'fundamental principles' prescribed in 1964 by the Ministry of Education (Ordinance No. 69) include, again as number one, the following aim: 'to assist the harmonious psychological and physical development of the child and to nurture the foundations for a healthy mind and body'.[7] The Japanese version of the last phrase includes the word *shinshin*, which combines the concepts mentioned above of 'body' and 'heart', here translated in the former case as 'mind'. In the case of kindergarten education, these aims may well have been influenced by the Froebelian ideal of 'a harmonious development of the whole person in his kindergarten world',[8] but I think that it is significant that the ideas of Froebel were so influential in Japan. The harmony of mind and body is also an important aim in the traditional martial arts, and oriental culture generally opposes this Cartesian opposition.

Hara and Wagatsuma, authors of a book entitled *Shitsuke,* go on to interpret the meaning even further in the light of other uses of the word, albeit written with different Chinese characters. One such use, usually included in the same dictionary entry as that concerned with child training, is a word translated into English as 'tacking' or 'basting', the stitching used to form the shape of a garment before it is sewn firmly, and, in the case of a kimono, to keep the garment in shape after it is sewn. Another use is concerned with the planting out of tiny rice seedlings, which must be placed upright in the soil and tended carefully to ensure a good mature plant. Other plants may be attended to in a special way when young, for example by removing certain shoots so that they will grow in a desired way, and this too is known as *shitsuke*. Hara and Wagatsuma thus interpret the concept to involve an element of construction, of 'making up' (*tsukurit-sukeru*), and also of 'straightening' (*tame*) into a desired character. As mentioned above, the phrase used for what is being 'made up' is 'one portion of a social person' or 'one member of society' and this word implies an eventual ability to contribute in an appropriate way to the society concerned. Thus Hara and Wagatsuma argue that *shitsuke* and teaching, taken together, make up the wider meaning of general education, which includes specific training in the art of living required by the particular occupational sphere to which the child belongs, not only in occupational skills, but also in the generally approved ways of life, morals and beliefs.[9] The character of the child is thus shaped in the way expected by society.

Other Japanese writers cite these different meanings of *shitsuke* in order to elucidate the concept of child-rearing. Makino has discussed the topic in English, where emphasis is again laid on the ethical and moral nuances as well as the 'training and practice of manners and etiquette' and the inculcation of basic ways of behaviour in daily life.[10] An article in Japanese by Aoi on the sociological approach to child rearing discusses other phrases associated with *shitsuke*, such as *kata ni hameru*, which means something like 'to fit into a mould', *kitaeru*, which may be translated 'to discipline', and a phrase which may be translated literally as 'the inculcation of habits without giving reasons' (*rikutsu nuki shūkanka saseru*).[11] The first phrase has taken on a rather derogatory meaning close to 'stereotyping' so that caretakers may say that it is something they wish to avoid, but essentially the concern is, like the last phrase, with the formation of habits. *Kitaeru* is used in the sense of 'to discipline', but it also means 'to forge' in the case of metal where it involves the heating, beating into shape, and strengthening by subsequent hardening of the object.

The business of child-rearing is thus associated with some of the most important elements of Japanese culture. Rice was the traditional staple of the Japanese people and its cultivators have always held a respected position in society. *Bonsai* and plants which characterise the famous Japanese garden are now in international demand. The traditional kimono has become an *objet d'art* in its own right as well as being admired as an elegant and beautiful garment. And the metalwork involved in the construction of Japanese swords and armour is a highly developed traditional skill appropriate for objects which symbolise some of the philosophy most basic to the Japanese way of life.[12] The creation of people is no less important to the continuity of the culture, and, in the Japanese case, is seen as another skill to be cultivated with a good deal of time and careful attention.

A child in the family

The emphasis placed on child-rearing is no doubt related to the high value children are accorded in other ways. A married couple without children is rare in Japan, and most families have their first child fairly soon after marriage. Those who delay are subjected to a veritable barrage of remarks and suggestions, as my husband and I discovered endlessly during my first period of research. It is also possible for a young couple to be addressed as 'mother' and 'father' before they even have any children. One of the chief purposes of marriage is often stated to be to have descendants; indeed, marriage itself is regarded much more as a matter of course in Japan than in some Western countries.[13]

This is part of the traditional ideology in Japan that a family is less a unit in its own right than part of a continuing entity known as the *ie* (house or household). This concept has been discussed in many works on Japan,[14] but the most relevant aspect in this context is that members of a house have a primary duty to the ancestors who went before them to provide descendants to follow on afterwards. Each generation is obliged to the previous one for its existence and upbringing and therefore expects to reciprocate by carrying out rites on behalf of the ancestors, caring for the living seniors in their old age, and providing for the subsequent generation.

In the post-war Constitution, drawn up during the Allied Occupation, this traditional system was legally abolished. Instead, families are to be created by two individuals on marriage, the new legal unit being the nuclear family formed by such a union. In practice many families do continue to follow the old principles to some extent. Descendants must be found to care for the ancestral tablets, and responsibilities between the generations seem to be taken seriously. In practice, this often involves the participation of grandparents in the rearing of their grandchildren. In many areas the continuing family also still exists as a residential unit, and even where this is not the case, there seems to be a preference for at least one child to remain as near as possible to the parents' home.

Even in the case of nuclear families, a marriage is seen as much more secure once children are born to the union. The celebration following the birth of a first child often includes all the important guests who attended the wedding and has been described as like a confirmation of the union.[15] A Japanese linguist, Takao Suzuki, has argued that this is because Japanese people prefer a relationship like that between parent and child which allows no room for free choice to the contractual type of relationship between husband and wife. Once a child is born, a husband and wife may see themselves as related more permanently through the 'natural' vertical relationship they each have with their child than they were through the previous 'chosen' horizontal role. Suzuki suggests that this is why they refer to one another more commonly as 'mother' and 'father' than in the 'saccharine' terms, such as 'honey' and 'darling' used by Americans ritually to reconfirm the contractual state of their type of marriage.[16]

Thus children in Japan have these important extra roles to play – to provide the vital continuity to the *ie*, until recently the basic unit of Japanese society, and to cement the relationship between the parents. However, the mere existence of children would be enough to fulfil these demands as long as the value of the house and its continuity can be inculcated in the new generation. The great emphasis placed on the rearing process has not yet been explained. After all, continuity is important in many societies, but some place much greater emphasis on the period of adolescence or initiation into adulthood than on the early period. Also, Japan is a country with a high abortion rate,[17] and, in times past, infanticide was common practice,[18] so it is evidently not just the physical child *per se* which is valued. It is no use giving birth if the subsequent care and attention is likely to be lacking. There are other collective ideas which contribute to the importance of child-rearing as well as just the provision of descendants.

Gifts of the gods

The child who now fits into the pre-school category was distinguished in some parts of Japan as still to some extent within the sphere of the divine world from which it was thought to have emerged. 'Until seven, amongst the gods' runs the saying,[19] and care was to be exercised with this special being. Much ritual and ceremony accompanies the first seven years of development, as will be described further in a later section, and this has been interpreted as originally due to the insecure state the child's soul was thought to be in at that time.[20] Children are also described as 'favours from the gods' and 'bestowed by the gods' and as such to be accorded appropriate care and attention. A more secular expression which recurs in songs and poetry is that 'there is no greater treasure than a child'.

A stark contrast between the collective view of this being and that of a child born into a Christian society is that there was no idea of original sin, or of a rebellious spirit which must be broken.[21] The Japanese say that a child has neither sin nor pollution,[22] indeed, it is even said to be a sin to make a child cry. A saying runs: 'you can win against neither the steward of the manor, nor a crying child'. The head of Shirayuri kindergarten emphasised several times that children are 'pure white' (*masshiro*) so that if they are naughty or difficult it is the fault of the teacher, or the misguided influence of the parents. Bad behaviour is blamed on some kind of outside agent, traditionally sometimes a type of insect (*kan no mushi*) which may be thought to have got in the child, making it cry a lot or act in an uncooperative way. In Kurotsuchi, for example, a young and otherwise rather 'modern' mother expecting her third baby explained the problems she was experiencing with the toilet training of her younger daughter to a *mushi* which she said was caused by the presence of a baby in her uterus. A child may even be taken to see a specialist to have such an affliction treated and there are apparently rites at both Shinto shrines and Buddhist temples for this purpose. Benedict reported that a priest may even go to the extent of removing the naughtiness in the form of a worm or insect;[23] elsewhere the practice is described as a rite of exorcism.[24] The notorious ultimate 'punishment' described by several Western writers – to burn a little *moxa* on a rebellious child's skin – is also said to be administered as a 'cure'.[25]

The soul of the three-year-o

In view of this approach, it is hardly surprising that t took greatly to their hearts the teachings of Froebel, who ...an's nature as good, and the bad side of child behaviour as due to a disturbed relationship between 'the true, original nature of a child and the distorted world of his environment'.[26] A book about the importance of child-rearing makes use of the Lockeian concept of the *tabula rasa* or 'white sheet' (*hakushi*) to describe the condition of a new born baby,[27] and, again, this fits very neatly with indigenous ideas. A white kimono was traditionally worn by a bride to symbolise the fresh start she was making in her new life and the eradication of the influence of her previous life, and white garments are worn by pilgrims, priests and the dead for similar reasons. The same symbolism underlies the nudity of 'naked festivals' and the intense activity at the end of each year to clear all debts and outstanding work so that a fresh start can be made each January.

In the case of a new-born baby, it is pointed out in the same book that there is an irreversible development of brain cells, eighty per cent of which are formed in the first three years of life, so that this is a wonderful opportunity to influence all future development.[28] This gleaning from science heavily influenced by the work of the American Glen Dovan, again fits in very neatly with an indigenous view, expressed in another saying, repeated constantly by caretakers and academics alike, that 'the soul of the three-year-old lasts till 100'. Thus great care and attention must be paid during these first vital years. A professor of education I heard speak to a group of some two-hundred mothers in a city hall in Kyushu reiterated the same argument, explaining that while animals rear by instinct, human beings have the chance to 'create' (*sōzō*) their children. A baby has limitless possible abilities, he coaxed, and it's up to their mothers and other caretakers to bring them out. This view may be rather extreme, and the Japanese are certainly aware of hereditary factors too, but they determine to bring out the best from the possible store. The head of Shirayuri insists that there is no such thing as a tone-deaf child, and as if to prove it, she trains every single one of her children to play in an eighty-piece orchestra at six years of age.

Thus, not only is a child essential to the well-being of the family

17

and valued as a treasure and gift to its caretakers, it also represents a responsibility for them to mould it in a way which will be acceptable to the wider society. The early period, when the child is largely in the hands of its mother and one or two other close relatives, is regarded as vitally important. The successful nature of this approach is perhaps illustrated in the results of some research carried out in the United States among first, second and third generation Japanese Americans. The investigators found that whereas the third generation Japanese had adopted many of the characteristics of their Caucasian counterparts, Japanese child-rearing practices tend to persist even through to this generation. This the author relates to continuing aspects of character found among Japanese Americans, in this case particularly likely to bring them success in American society. Thus the caretakers seem to have adapted their methods to fit the society of their adoption – or, possibly, the early period prepares them anyway for successful adaptation.[29]

One final piece of support for the importance of the early period has been pointed out by Takeo Doi, the well-known Japanese psychiatrist. He has written at length about aspects of character which he regards as peculiar to the Japanese, and, in particular, he claims that there is a 'fundamental emotional urge' for *amae*, translated into English somewhat clumsily as 'dependency', which has fashioned the Japanese for some two-thousand years.[30] This 'dependency', which is entirely necessary for babies, is, according to Doi, encouraged to persist throughout adult life in Japan, whereas in the Western approach, independence is encouraged from an early age. This opposition has been a dominant theme in the psychological comparisons of Japan and the United States. Doi cites the case of the Japanese emperor as a supreme example of the status accorded 'infantile dependence' in that society. The Emperor expects those around him to make all decisions, deal with problems, and take over the government, but he still retains his superior status. 'He is no different from a babe in arms, yet his rank is the highest in the land'.[31] So ingrained is this aspect of Japanese character, Doi writes, that it was only after defeat in the Second World War that he suddenly realised that 'the essence of the Japanese experience lies in the period of infancy'.[32]

The expectation of attention for children

Various practical aspects of the usual Japanese approach to child care illustrate the amount of attention expected from the adults involved. These will be discussed in more detail in subsequent chapters, but some apparently persistent practices may be mentioned briefly here. In view of the influence from the West, and the interest taken in Western practices by Japanese mothers, it is quite revealing to comment on some areas where practices remain very different. The examples chosen probably reflect a somewhat ethnocentric view, but the reactions of Japanese caretakers to my own approach were often as revealing of their attitudes as were direct observations of their practices. Thus, the shock expressed by one informant who, on visiting England, observed a three-month-old baby being put down to sleep in a cot in its own room, encouraged an investigation of the expectations which were being undermined. Similarly, the fact that play pens have been introduced in Japan, but largely rejected, seems to indicate another area of possibly fruitful investigation. It is also interesting to examine some of the Western theories of child psychology which are apparently being steadfastly ignored.

Bedtime

In the case of cots, it is not the appliance itself which is rejected since many Japanese households now use them for babies. Rather, it is the way in which they are used which is different. Traditionally, mothers took babies into their own bedding or provided a small mattress beside their own for a young child. The possibility of suffocation if a tiny baby shares an adult's bed has been taken seriously, but it is nevertheless thought to be important that a mother or other caretaker be close at hand to attend to a baby's needs. Thus a cot will usually be placed next to an adult's bed or mattress. It is also usually customary for an adult to lull a baby to sleep before placing it in the

19

cot, and to pick it up again if it should wake up, since it is said to be important that the baby experience as little anxiety as possible.

When the child grows up a little, it is usual for a caretaker to lie down beside it at bedtime until it falls asleep.[33] This can be a time-consuming process, and there are two basic ways in which a busy mother deals with the problem. The first is to strap the child to her back so that it can nap there while she keeps her hands free for other tasks, and this is a custom still commonly observed in Japan, despite the introduction of push-chairs which are also used to ferry small children about. If a child is able to play happily in the evening, the mother's other response to the problem of finding time to lie down with her child at bedtime is to keep it up until she herself is ready to go to bed. A study of kindergarten entry forms revealed an ideal bedtime for children somewhat later than that found in England, although it probably compares better with the United States and continental Europe, but mothers who discussed this subject in interviews often pointed out that in practice a child would stay up later than the time they named, since they regarded it as more important to have time to settle the child calmly than to stick rigidly to the decided hour. It is also true, however, that children often fall asleep in front of the television, or sitting with some other member of the family, when they may merely be transferred to their cot or other sleeping place.

Ideally, then, the mother will lie down at the appropriate time with

Table 1: Reported bedtimes

	7p.m.	8p.m.	9p.m.	10p.m.	11p.m.	Total no. children
Shirayuri Kindergarten Household information	8	27	57	27	6	125
Tateyama Kindergarten Household information	6	95	176	51	4	332
Interview families which had a fixed bedtime	1	3	16	10	1	31

her child until it falls asleep, after which she might have some time to herself. In practice, this time seems to be rather short, if it exists at all, and the system is a far cry from the arrangements in England and other Western countries, where a baby is put into its own room as soon as possible so that its parents can enjoy some free time together. The employment of baby sitters so that parents of small children may go out together in the evenings is another Western custom which is known and largely rejected in Japan. Mothers may leave quite tiny babies with neighbours or other members of the family for short periods during the day, but an evening out with one's husband is evidently not thought of as a priority warranting the introduction of a relative stranger into a baby or child's life at the time when it should be settling down to sleep. In theory, in three-generation households, a couple could leave children with their grandparents, but, especially in more traditional areas, the husband and wife anyway have little social life together, and, indeed, some informants laughed at the very idea.[34] Even in cities, couples with otherwise quite Westernised lifestyles seem not to regard their own social life as important once they have begun to have children.

Indeed, the needs of the child are still paramount during the night and many children share an adult's bed until kindergarten age or older.[35] Even when they are deemed old enough to have their own bedding, this is usually laid out beside that of the parents, many of whom describe the way their children creep under their covers during the course of the night. One common arrangement is apparently to have a child sleep between its parents, and this is described by the Chinese character for river (川), which is written with a short vertical stroke between two longer ones. In theory, an older child is supposed to sleep with its father once a new baby is born, but more than one mother reported that she habitually slept with all the children so that her husband could get a good night's sleep. In three-generation households, one or more of the children may sleep with their grandparents, but this may also be quite flexible, so that children are allowed to decide each night with whom they will sleep. Again, the important factor is that the child should not experience any anxiety.

The rejection of the playpen

The rejection of the playpen reflects a difference of approach to caring for babies during their active periods. In the West, these contraptions may be used to provide a safe area in which a baby can play with its toys and amuse itself while adults attend to other matters. Larger areas may be 'child-proofed' by removing precious or dangerous objects allowing the baby freedom to explore, again relatively unhindered and unhindering to adults. In Japan the playpen was apparently regarded as too much like a prison, anyway rather superfluous since babies are where possible accompanied by attentive adults while they play and explore. A mother too busy to provide such attention would probably strap a baby to her back to keep it out of trouble, but if it were playing on the floor, there would usually be someone there beside it pointing out things that are safe to play with and diverting its attention from those that are dangerous and precious. Thus babies are often seen playing only a few feet from a priceless vase or a beautiful flower arrangement, learning if they show an interest that these are perhaps grandmother's special things. Grandmother may even allow a little hand to touch them carefully, but then she will deftly introduce something more interesting to the infant so that no harm ensues. The child is thought to need guidance even in its first explorations. In subsequent chapters it will be illustrated that there are specific aims involved.

In fact, Japan had its own traditional version of the playpen, a straw basket called an *ejiko,* which enclosed a baby entirely. This was used in some regions by farming families who had to make use of their entire adult work force at busy times for economic reasons. In some cases, the babies were even left alone in the family home while the adults went out to the fields.[36] As the child grew, it might be tied to a tree so that it could play within a confined area, it was reported by an informant who grew up in the north of Japan (Tōhoku). A contraption with wheels, which encloses a baby but gives it the chance to push itself around, has recently been imported from Japan to England, though the Japanese have now rejected it as bad for the development of leg muscles. Such aids may go against the ideals, but the principles of full-time care are not destroyed because practical difficulties sometimes make them impossible to carry out. It would be pointless to give undivided attention to a child for whom there was no food.

Holding out

One area where Western and Japanese theories of child psychology are at present quite different is in the approach to toilet training,[37] and this also seems to be related to the amount of attention an adult is expected to give to babies and small children. It seems to be fairly common practice in Europe and the United States to change a baby's napkins at regular intervals, or when it is very dirty, and to leave the business of potty training until the child is in its second or third year. Indeed, it is these days even said to be positively detrimental to start trying to train a child too early, although the reasons for this seem to vary from one book or manual to another. In Japan the advice is quite different and depends on a very close relationship between caretaker and child. Many informants reported that while a baby is still in napkins, they change it every time it is wet, which gradually gives them a good idea of its natural rhythms. As early as a few weeks in some cases, but anyway in the summer after or near the child's first birthday, the caretaker begins trying to anticipate the baby's needs. The child is held in a distinctive way, or taken to a potty, and the same onomatapoeic words are repeated (*shishi* for urine, *unun* for bowel evacuation) so that eventually it learns to ask itself. The principles are simple, but a great deal of time and dedication are required to achieve success, as I learnt to my cost when I put my eighteen-month-old off potties altogether by trying 'to go native'. My next door neighbour, meanwhile, was hardly washing a napkin for a baby only a few months old. She claimed that he had emptied his bowels regularly every morning at 6 a.m. since he was two months old. We left before he celebrated his first birthday and he was already wearing underpants. I think this case was unusual, even in Japan, but most informants agreed with the method, and another claimed that her daughter of twelve months could even ask for the toilet when she wanted to go. From the household information provided by parents entering their children in Tateyama Kindergarten, the average age at which children were reported able to ask before urinating was just under twenty months, with a range from ten months to 3 years.

Some families in the country explained that the pressure of farm work made it difficult for them to conform to the ideal. In Kurotsuchi it was often a grandfather who was entrusted with the care of a small child, and mothers did not seem to expect them to attend to such matters. However, most babies were held out when their napkins were changed from a few months, and were often trained quite early if a grandmother, rather than a grandfather, were in sole charge. The principles of training were much the same, and practical difficulties were explained as deviances.

General availability

The general expectation of an adult's availability, if not always actual presence, seems to continue as the child grows up a little. Kindergartens have rather short hours and take odd days off from time to time for a variety of reasons including an annual visit by teachers to each child's house. They also hold open days when mothers or grandmothers may come and observe proceedings. In fact there were often special activities for that day, some of which involved the participation of the visiting adult, so that children whose mothers were too busy to attend were left out. At schools, too, such open days are held once a month and mothers who have jobs apparently feel under pressure to take time off to attend them. In the kindergarten case, these open days are part of a programme of education for parents, which also includes lectures on topics such as home education, health, discipline and child psychology.[38] There is also usually a PTA which organises activities such as bazaars, outings and other social events, and, for private kindergartens, raises a good deal of their income. In Japan such groups are not always concerned with educational policy, but active and generous participation can apparently be related to a child's selection for concert appearance and so forth.

Much of the previous paragraph may be little different from a description of a situation in England or the United States, and since kindergartens have been introduced directly from the West, this is hardly surprising. The Western middle-class expectation of a mother who has no need to go out to work has also some influence in Japan, but the point being emphasised here is rather different. A Western mother with time on her hands generally becomes involved in voluntary work or at least an active social life, possibly even hiring a nanny to take care of her children, whereas a non-working Japanese mother often centres her whole life around her children and their progress. The point is perhaps better illustrated by considering the extent of a mother's involvement in other classes available for small children. One popular activity in 1981 was music lessons organised by Yamaha, during which their electone organs are used. Mothers are expected to sit by the child throughout the lesson, to help them follow the teacher's instructions and to guide their fingers in playing the instrument. This way a large number of children may be taught by one teacher, and no doubt a large number of electone sales are eventually clocked up too. The principles of parental participation are also found elsewhere, however, as is widely known in the internationally successful Suzuki schools for teaching the violin to small children. Even in *kendō* classes, where children from the age of four are trained in this martial art, mothers need to be present or close by so that after an initial training period they can help their children put on the special clothes and head-dresses which must be worn for the mock battles which ensue.

Even as children prepare for school, few mothers seem to feel that they can leave education to the specialists. Salesmen make routine house-to-house visits before the start of each school year trying to sell sets of books which are designed to help mothers keep abreast of what is currently on the curriculum. An article in the *Japan Times*[39] quoted a letter from a reader complaining about the pressure put on her by such salesmen, who apparently point out that if a child were sick for a week he would miss vital material and perhaps be unable to catch up, suggesting that it was the responsibility of the mother, rather than the teacher, to see that he did. The reader had remarked, perhaps a little cynically, that school was evidently not a place where children learn and gain important knowledge, as she had thought, but rather where they are evaluated on the learning they have done at home and in classes after school.

Certainly most of the mothers I interviewed reported that their children are able to read the simple phonetic characters before they enter school in their seventh year, although few kindergartens formally teach this skill, and head teachers at primary schools assured me that a pupil who started completely unable to read would usually catch up with the others by the second year. Some mothers said that their children learned their characters 'naturally', or by watching television, but many also played games involving reading practice with them, and some gave considerable time to helping their pre-school children achieve a degree of literacy. One mother whose five-year-old apparently showed no interest in learning characters said that she was very worried in case he would fall behind on starting school, still a year away. Since school is, in Japan as elsewhere, the place where children are taught to read, this mother's concern seems to be indicative of social pressure generated by the expectations of mothers themselves. Table 2 indicates the numbers of children reported able to read and write at Shirayuri Kindergarten at different ages, and a 1972 national survey found that 87.9% of five-year-olds could read at least sixty characters,[40] despite the fact that school doesn't start until the seventh year.

Public concern

In the collective view that a child was said to be a gift of the gods, it was also sometimes thought that it started life with the benefit of a certain amount of supernatural power which worked not only through its parents but also through the other people surrounding it.[41] The community in which a child was born was responsible for certain aspects of its rearing, and every member of that community was expected to look after and care for the child when the occasion arose. Some evidence of this idea is still observable in neighbourhoods and villages where children are allowed to play in the streets and footpaths from a very early age, their mothers relying on the responsibility their neighbours will surely feel should their children run into difficulties. In Kurotsuchi, neighbours attend the presentation of a new baby to the local shrine, which often coincides with the mother's return to her village of adoption on marriage from that

Table 2: Literacy skills at Shirayuri Kindergarten

	Reading			Writing		
Age	Yes	No	A little	Yes	No	A little
3–4	15	21		5	29	2
4–5	39	15	4	22	28	8
5–6	46	4	1	42	7	2

of her natal family where she goes for the birth. On one such occasion, the mother's own mother was present and the villagers, who gathered to see the baby, thanked her for taking care of their new member at this early stage of his life, expressing a kind of collective ownership and responsibility for the child.[42]

Hara and Wagatsuma have pointed out that with the use of contraceptives and birth control nowadays children may be regarded as 'made' (tsukurimono), rather than 'bestowed' by the gods (sazukarimono), but they leave open the question of whether the old ideology has been replaced by the idea that children are the parents' property only.[43] The responsibility falls particularly heavily on parents in nuclear families. There has been a tremendous shift from the support of the continuing family and, indeed, the whole community, to the rather isolated situation of mothers in the vastly increased numbers of nuclear families in modern cities. A Japanese sociologist discussing this shift has pointed out that in modern nuclear families parents lack confidence in their child-rearing practices.[44] During a television programme in the summer of 1981 on the subject of child-rearing, results were announced of a survey carried out in Tokyo and Osaka, which indicated that some forty per cent of women interviewed had no confidence in their own rearing practices.

In an article about the relationship between juvenile delinquency and home training, Makino and his colleagues discussed in 1970 the attitude that too much was now left to the nuclear family and suggested that there be a move to revive the public aspect of child training, to entrust part of the 'home training' to kindergartens and schools, and to unify disciplinary training and moral education in the programme of public education.[45] In fact, in 1981, there seemed to be a good deal of public concern about the importance of the early period in a child's development. In the first place, child-rearing is a topic which provokes intense interest on a theoretical level in a wide range of Japanese people. The majority of fathers seem to have little time available for their own small children, but men as well as women, perhaps even more than women, express strong views on the subject. They frequently quote the saying, for example, that the soul of a three-year-old will last till 100, so the first three years of life are of vital importance. A head of the Sony Corporation, Masaru Ibuka, apparently a friend of the Suzuki after whom the early violin learning method is named, wrote a complete book on this topic entitled *Kindergarten Is Too Late*.

There is also a nationwide programme of Parent Education Guidance subsidised by the Ministry of Education, Science and Culture. This includes lectures for young and expectant mothers arranged by local departments of education and welfare. In one such class, in Yame City in Kyushu, a university professor of education had been invited to speak to an enormous gathering of perhaps two hundred women, several accompanied by small, quite noisy children. The speaker used strong local dialect and evidently appealed to the mothers in the frequent use of jokes and asides. He was congenial and charming, but at another such talk in Tateyama City, a headmaster who was only introducing the speaker took it upon himself to admonish the mothers present for neglecting their duties. It seemed a little strange to me that it should almost always be men who lecture to women on the role to which the latter give so much more of their own time, especially since women are highly educated in Japan, but a female psychologist, herself a mother and a university lecturer, told me that she was convinced most mothers would attach more weight to a talk from a man than from someone like herself with the same qualifications. This phenomenon perhaps reflects the lack of confidence women have in their own methods, but also indicates that men have a role to play too, if only at a theoretical level.

Other aspects of the national programme include special television

28

shows about infant education and a system of postcard correspondence sent out to parents with advice on practices appropriate to the ages of their children. These include invitations to attend further classes, and apparently in 1978 some 650,000 parents responded to such programmes.[46] In 1981 the Tateyama department of education was initiating a series of classes for mothers of kindergarten children, and planned soon to run such a course for newly-married women. Various booklets, published by prefectural offices of education and welfare, are issued to pregnant mothers and those who bring their children for routine check-ups. Detailed advice is given not only on diet, health and safety, but also on ideals and techniques of training. Many of the values considered important emerge in such booklets and these will be discussed further in Chapters III and IV. Similar publications are issued by drug companies and other interested firms, and are made readily available, usually free. Bookshops, too abound in books and magazines on similar topics. Much of what they advocate is remarkably consistent from one publication to another, which contrasts with such works available in many Western countries.

On a more practical level, the Ministry of Health and Welfare has developed a comprehensive range of child welfare services, particularly since the Child Welfare Law of 1947 and the Maternal and Child Health Law of 1965.[47] Pregnant mothers are required to register at their local health centre where they may be examined free of charge. They receive a 'pocketbook', which contains advice about pregnancy, childbirth and upbringing, and in which a record is kept of their own health, the birth, and the health of the child once it is born. Public health nurses and midwives conduct home visits during pregnancy and soon after the baby is born, especially where families are experiencing problems. For example, low-income families receive free milk for a period of nine months. All children under six years of age are provided by law with vaccinations for smallpox, diphtheria, whooping cough and polio, as well as a BCG innoculation against tuberculosis. At three years, children are called to attend a medical, dental and psychological examination during which early disorders may be detected and treatment recommended. I attended one such examination day in Tateyama, when long lines of mothers and children waited in a huge civic centre to sit their often protesting child in front of a dentist and a doctor, then to discuss their child's progress with a public health nurse. The examination, which began at 1.30 p.m., was so efficiently conducted that the half-dozen doctors and dentists were leaving at 2.15 p.m. having seen a couple of hundred children. Nurses in charge of the proceedings explained that only two to three per cent of mothers fail to attend, and these receive a home visit to ascertain the reason. Since 1977 a similar routine check-up has been held at eighteen months, organised at a municipal rather than national level.[48]

Local welfare departments have consultation facilities for families with problems, and a variety of services available to help them. Financial aid may be provided in severe cases, and, as well as homes for orphans and handicapped children, there are also a large number of day nurseries to cater for the children of working mothers. All these facilities have come to be taken rather for granted in England and some other European countries, but in a country like Japan, where the welfare system is relatively poorly developed, this emphasis on child care seems to be another indication of the public concern for children.

Public day nurseries were first established in 1918 in Japan, rising to sixty-five throughout the country by 1926, when there were already 228 private ones.[49] During the Second World War, the demand increased to accommodate the children of mothers working for wartime needs, and since 1947 the total number of private and public day nurseries has increased from under two thousand to 22,709 in 1982. These cater for over two million children.[50] In large urban areas the situation is said to be different, but in cities such as Yame and Tateyama, where I carried out research, there were places available for all the working mothers who applied, either in public nurseries or in private ones registered with the municipal authorities. These generally open during normal working hours, some of them providing facilities for school children between the end of school and the time their parents finish work. In large cities there are also a number of private establishments operating around the clock to accommodate the babies and infants of women who work at night, but these 'baby hotels' have come in for a good deal of criticism for failing to meet national standards of space and number of caretakers. The news value accorded such an issue could be seen as another indication of general public concern for children.

It should be pointed out also that these public facilities are not intended to remove ultimate responsibility for children's upbringing from their families. Despite the apparent ease with which a mother going out to work may arrange alternative care for her infants, this is not a measure which is widely approved of. Traditionally most mothers were engaged in economically productive activities in Japan, so this is not a new development, but since they used to live in three-generation households, a grandparent would be available to attend to the children while the mother was out. Alternatively, the mother would be involved in a household occupation so that she could divide her time between work at home and the care of her children. Such arrangements, which are still found in many families, seem generally to be preferred as better for the children. The number of day nurseries has increased along with the number of nuclear families separated from their senior generations. Their purpose is stated clearly to be to provide for children whose families lack sufficient care.[51]

Even heads of day nurseries whom I interviewed expressed the view that their charges would be better off at home. One female head, herself a mother who had left her own children with a neighbour's family when they were small, said that she had heard that some girls brought up in day nurseries are unable to feed their own babies when they grow up. Another reported that some of the mothers who leave their children with her in the daytime collect them for their tea, bathe them, and deliver them to a private child minder for the night when they go out to work. She said that such people would be better off not to have any children, and that people in Japan generally feel that children should be at home until they are three, or at least while they are babies.[52] In fact, most day nurseries only cater for babies once they are weaned on to solid food, so that alternative arrangements have to be found for the early period anyway. Employers are obliged by law to provide only six weeks' maternity leave before and after the birth, with thirty minutes off twice a day for feeding until the baby is one year old,[53] but many companies now provide more time. Some municipal and other employees can take off a year without pay to attend to their babies during the early period. However, it is also said that many companies expect their female employees to leave when they marry or have babies,[54] which reflects the general view that mothers should be at home when their children are small.

Mothers with children in day nurseres were aware of this disapproval. Some justified themselves by saying that they liked their work and wanted to keep it up. In Japan, as elsewhere, there is a growing feeling amongst women that they have been expected to give up too much, but equally, in country districts, some mothers resent being expected to continue working while their mothers-in-law have time at home to look after the children. The comment of a mother at home with her children was couched in terms which are relevant to the Japanese view of children: she complained that they are too much at the centre of the family, which gives a mother no chance to do anything for herself. This reflects the general idea that a small child needs full-time care. Thus, a grandmother who has adopted this role may well expect her daughter-in-law to come home from a full day's work outside to cook the evening meal as well as dealing with the cleaning and the family wash, so that the child can benefit from the grandmother's uninterrupted attention.

After the age of three, children are expected to attend some form of public institution to make friends and experience group life in preparation for school. Kindergartens, administered by the local education departments, under the guidance of the Ministry of Education, are now available in most areas for children from the age of three or four until they enter primary school in their seventh year. The cost to parents is very small. After a slow start, when they were first introduced into Japan in 1876, their number increased gradually during the early part of this century, and, again, mushroomed after the Second World War to be catering for a total of 2,193,000 children in 15,190 establishments in 1983.[55] Nearly all children now attend a kindergarten or day nursery before they enter school, which, although voluntary, seems to be regarded as an important part of early education.

Public kindergarten teachers visit each child's home at least once a year to try and establish a degree of co-operation with the parents of their charges, but also to get to know them better and understand their home situation. They go more often if children are sick or have problems. This is part of the general reponsibility teachers are expected to have for their pupils even outside the context of the kindergarten itself. In one class I attended, a teacher was lecturing her four- and five-year-olds one day because she had noticed while walking through their neighbourhood the previous evening that some of them were still playing outside at 6 p.m. She suggested that the children make promises with their parents to be home earlier than this. Before the same children went home that day, she reminded them that they should change their clothes when they arrived home since the hot weather they were experiencing at that time of year made them very sweaty.

At the end of term in another kindergarten, the headmistress gave the children a talk on how they should spend their free time during the summer holidays. She advised them against watching too much television or eating too many sweets, indeed against going to play too much in other people's houses. She told them to get up early in the morning, go to bed early in the evening, to be careful of cars, and to refrain from asking their parents or other relatives for too many things when they were taken to festivals. In case her words were forgotten, each child was given a 'Summer Life' book, with ideas for activities, spaces to record them with little coloured stickers, and a repetition of important points to remember about their behaviour. Notes were provided in the margin for the guidance of the mother.[56]

Dentists visit the kindergartens as part of the public health service, as do doctors to adminster non-compulsory innoculations. In contrast to the situation at the three-year check-up, when many children protested violently, the dental examination and vaccinations at the kindergarten were carried out in complete calm. The children waited quietly in an orderly queue, clutching their own records carefully, ready to be handed over to the secretary as they presented themselves submissively for whatever was the order of the day. Some suggestions about how this change of heart is achieved will emerge in Chapter V.

A final indication of the public concern for pre-school children in Japan is to be found in the positive wealth of parks and playgrounds available for their use in even the largest of cities although it should be noted that these are often very small by international standards. It was a boast of the administration of Tokyo's governor Minobe that they planned to create 579 playgrounds so that there would be one within 100 metres of every family by the early 1970s. This was part of a plan to improve living standards and welfare provisions for Tokyo residents, known as the 'civic minimum', which apparently struck a responsive chord in the Tokyo electorate and played an important part in the 1971 election when Minobe won with a huge majority of more than one and a half million votes.[57] National subsidies are also provided to support children's indoor halls and some children's clubs, and further plans are under way to construct 'an indoor comprehensive institution for children's sound growth' in urban areas.[58]

Ceremony, symbolism and religious support

The privileged place accorded small children in Japanese society is emphasised on a ritual level in ceremonies associated with their development, and in wider religious activities. Many Shinto festivals, held throughout Japan, have a special part for children, sometimes said to be associated with their supposed proximity to the deities.[59] It would also not be an exaggeration to say that more life cycle ceremonies are associated with the early period of childhood than with any other stage. These vary regionally, though there are some which seem to be found in most parts of the country and others which have recently been standardised nationally.[60] A consideration of some of the popular ones will illustrate the point.

Celebrations of development

The first celebration takes place during pregnancy, when the mother begins to wrap herself in a long piece of corseting which she continues to wear until about a month after the baby is born. Most mothers wear this *obi*, sometimes received as a gift from their own families, from about five months into their term. If a celebration is held, it takes place on a dog day, according to the Chinese calendar, because dogs are said to have an easy delivery. Typically a few relatives will gather to share a meal and drink to the health of the mother and child. Rice cakes may also be distributed to the neighbours and more distant relatives, which makes the occasion a kind of public announcement of the expected birth. The same neighbours and relatives may well take gifts when the child is born. At the same time, the expectant mother and her own mother may also visit a shrine to pray for an easy delivery.[61]

Nowadays the birth itself usually takes place in hospital under sterile conditions, but the umbilical cord is carefully preserved and placed in a special box, which the mother takes home with her. Some private hospitals also provide a glossy photograph of the mother and baby as part of their service.

On about the seventh day after birth, there is a ceremony which has a number of regional variations, but essentially seems to be associated with the naming of the child. It is sometimes called the 'seventh night' (*shichiya*), but more commonly recognised as a naming ceremony (*meimei*), which may actually be held any time during the two weeks allowed for registration of the birth. Details vary, but the child's name is usually written out on a special piece of paper which is then hung up in a place of honour in the house. The two sets of grandparents may share a meal to celebrate this occasion, which nowadays also sometimes coincides with the return of the mother and child from hospital.

The first presentation of a new baby to the local Shinto shrine is held at different times in different areas, commonly a month after birth, but in some areas as long as fifty or even a hundred days afterwards. This may represent the end of a period when the mother is regarded as polluted and therefore unable to enter the shrine, but in Tateyama the pollution period ended earlier than this and was marked by a distribution of small gifts of thanks to neighbours and relatives who brought gifts to the baby at birth. At the shrine there may be a small ceremony performed by the local priest to pray for the child's health, or the mother and grandmother may just lay the child before the altar and make it cry so that the deity will be aware of its new parishioner. Many babies are dressed in an elaborate kimono for this ceremony, a garment which is often presented by the maternal grandparents. In Kurotsuchi it is customary to call on a relative or neighbour on the way home from this visit, where a spot of ink for a boy, and lipstick for a girl, is put on the head of the baby, said to wish success in the future. In a rural part of Chiba prefecture a couple is chosen to act as sponsor for the baby, to take responsibility for it until the age of seven, and this couple attends all subsequent celebrations for the child.

The next ceremony marks ritually the start of the weaning process, when the baby is given its first tiny taste of solid food. This takes place 100 days after birth, in some areas 110 or 120, or an auspicious day near to that time. A tray is laid before the baby, on which is arranged a bowl of soft-boiled rice, a special fish, and a pair of brand new chopsticks with which the baby is served a taste of the food. Sometimes soup and other dishes are included, perhaps having symbolic meaning. For example, one type of fish used has a name which changes as it gets bigger, the overall name having a homonym meaning 'success' (*shusseuo*), served to the child in the hope that it will grow, like the fish, through all the stages of its life with success. Three small pebbles may also be placed on a dish to symbolise the hope that the child's milk teeth, which are about to appear, will grow strong like the stone. In Tateyama some parents combined this occasion with the first visit to the Shinto shrine.

These two 'firsts' are practiced widely throughout Japan, the visit to a shrine being replaced by one to a temple for families who have exclusive allegiances, for example to the 'new' Buddhist sect known as Soka Gakkai. However, there were many other small 'first' ceremonies in the past, some still practised in the regions, associated with such things as the first bath, first clothes, first outing, first hair-cut and first bridge-crossing. One current custom reported from Chiba prefecture was the baking of large white rice cakes on the third day after birth as a charm to ensure that the mother has plenty of milk for the baby. In Kurotsuchi the first New Year after a baby's birth is marked by the presentation from the grandparents of expensive gifts: a bow and arrow for a boy, a 'badminton racket' decorated with a beautiful cloth doll for a girl, both enclosed in glass cases to be displayed in the best room of the house.

An occasion which is remembered throughout Japan, especially for a first child (and, if necessary, first son), is the first *sekku*, celebrated on 'girls' day', 3 March, for girls, and on 'boys' day', 5

May, for boys. This may well involve a sizeable gathering of relatives, compared by some informants to the wedding ceremony, and, again, the receipt of expensive, decorative gifts. In the house of a baby girl a miniature representation of the sumptuous Imperial Court of the Heian period (ninth to twelfth centuries AD) is set out on tiered shelves. It displays dolls dressed in the ceremonial costume of the time, palanquins, lanterns and trays containing tiny feasts. Their splendour is said to be to inspire girls to emulate the traditional elegance of the highest family in the land. Although, of course, a baby is not aware of the detail of this gift when it is first received, she sees it again each year when it is customarily set up for girls' day. For boys the arrangement includes samurai armour and helmets, arrows, and dolls depicting historical and mythological characters who displayed courage and other qualities deemed desirable for a boy to acquire. These, too are set up once a year, and both provide regular reminders of objects of cultural importance, and opportunities for children to picture and imagine historical stories they may have heard at home or in kindergarten. Outside, above the house, for boys huge cloth carp streamers fly in the springtime wind proclaiming the presence of sons to the world at large. Carp are chosen because they are said to swim against the current, thus displaying strength in adversity, another quality it is hoped that the baby will absorb. Special food is also prepared on this occasion, some wrapped in leaves which again symbolise aspirations for the development of the child.

Birthday parties have become popular in Japan in recent years, but this is a Western influence and they usually follow Western lines, including a cake with candles and a gathering of friends who dress up and bring gifts. The baby's first birthday is sometimes celebrated in a special way, however, especially if it has learned to walk before that time. This is said to be an inauspicious accomplishment since it suggests that the child will wander away when it grows up, so a large rice cake, or a bag of rice, is tied to the precocious baby's back to make it fall down. In Kurotsuchi, a large, flat rice cake is laid on the floor and the baby made to take steps over it. At the other side it finds various objects on a tray. Depending on the object it chooses to pick up first, predictions are made about its future. If a baby picks up a purse, it will be rich, if a pen, it will be a writer . . . and so on.

There is a national celebration on 15 November, or in some areas the nearest auspicious day, when boys of three and five, and girls of three and seven, are taken to shrines in fine clothes for rites of protection and prayers for good fortune in the future. This is actually an amalgamation of previous rites held in different social classes and different areas for 'first' hair-styles and 'first' wearing of particular garments. Nowadays girls are dressed in kimono and boys in either a smart Western suit or a traditional Japanese garment. In Kurotsuchi the children were merely taken to the shrine for the appropriate rite, but in Tateyama this is the occasion for another large gathering of relatives and even neighbours in many families. Rice with beans, a dish to denote celebration, is taken to neighbours, many of whom give the child a gift of money. This is also regarded as a landmark sufficiently important to call in a professional photographer to record the occasion in a large, glossy hard-back print, to be kept carefully with those of the parents' wedding. One family I interviewed had been posted to Greece for the period during which their daughter became three, so they dressed her up in a kimono on 15 November and took her to the Athenian Acropolis in lieu of the shrine.

Although the national celebration on 15 November is called the 7–5–3 celebration (*shichi-go-san*), it is interesting that some people omit the fifth year and make a particular occasion of the third and seventh. These are ages regarded as particularly important in a child's development since, as has already been mentioned, 'the soul of the three year old lasts till 100' and 'until seven, amongst the gods' coincide approximately with entry into school and kindergarten respectively. There are other ways, too, in which these ages are seen as important landmarks, and historical evidence suggests that they have been marked ceremonially for as long as there are records, whereas the celebration associated with the fifth year was less firmly fixed.[62] In Kurotsuchi, it was in fact the seventh-year ceremony which was sometimes omitted, but since this now coincides with entry into primary school, it seems to be adequately marked with a celebration of that event (*nyūgakushiki*).

In general, continuing families were rather more punctilious in carrying out these ceremonies than nuclear ones, though many young couples told me that their parents reminded them about the specific occasions of their own children,[63] often sending money or expensive garments for the children to wear. It seems to depend on the family whether a large gathering will be held, but some influence seems to be found in the practices of neighbours, since it is difficult to avoid reciprocity in these matters. Some nuclear families who had no intention of bothering with such 'old-fashioned' practices end up celebrating most of the occasions because it seems to be expected in the neighbourhood.

Table 3: Ceremonies held for children (from interview sample)

Ceremony	Tateyama/Tokyo			Kyushu		
	Yes	No	Not yet	Yes	No	Not yet
Celebration during pregnancy	24	3		22		
Naming ceremony (or seventh night)	22	5		20	2	
First shrine visit (miyamairi)	24	3		22		
Ritual weaning (kuizome)	21	6		20	2	
Osekku	27			22		
First birthday (traditional)	10	1		20		2
(modern party)	16					
7–5–3 (shichi-go-san)	25	1	1	16		6

Further life-crisis ceremonies are rare and considerably simpler than those held during this early period of childhood. There is a rite in some areas at thirteen, again involving special garments, but this is far from widely practised. After their twentieth birthday all young people in Japan officially become adults, a status ritually conferred at a ceremony held publically throughout Japan on 15 January each year. Again, this occasion involves new and expensive clothes. Some years in the life cycle are regarded as particularly vulnerable, and adults may visit Shinto shrines for purification ceremonies rather similar to those held for children at three, five and seven, but this is practised by very few people compared with those who take their children at the appropriate ages. Finally, during old age, there are certain times of celebration: at sixty, when one cycle of the Chinese calendar is complete, and at some or all of seventy, seventy-seven, eighty, eighty-eight, ninety and a hundred, with regional variations. At the close of life, then, the celebrations seem to bunch together again, but few live to see them all, and even if they do, the occasions never seem to reach quite the frequency and fuss accorded the development of the pre-school child. This case contrasts with societies which place ritual emphasis on the period of adolescence, or initiation into adulthood, for example, a situation which is commonly found in Africa and other areas.[64]

Annual events

There are also a number of annual events which involve small children. The gifts received at the first *sekku* are set up each year for a period preceding the appropriate days, as already mentioned. These 'boys' days' and 'girls' days' are two of the five festivals which used to be held in Japan on the first day of the first lunar month, the third of the third month (now girls' day), the fifth of the fifth month (now boys' day), the seventh of the seventh and the ninth of the ninth lunar months of each year. These were officially cancelled in 1873,[65] but New Year is still the most important national holiday of the year, when children may be at the centre of the celebrations; 5 May has been made a national holiday, known as Children's Day; 3 March is celebrated as girls' day in homes throughout the land, and Tanabata, that festival traditionally held on the seventh of the seventh month, is still often celebrated wherever there are children. It could well be that this feast has been revived in recent years since it was reported in 1910 that it was rarely celebrated in Tokyo,[66] whereas now it seems to be a time chosen for young children all over the land to practise their calligraphy.

According to an old fairy tale of Chinese origin, the night of Tanabata is the only one during the year when the two stars Vega and Altair, known as the celestial princess weaver and her cowherd lover, may meet. The tale has it that the couple fell in love, and, although they were allowed to marry, they spent too much time with each other and neglected their work of weaving and herding. Thus, the weaver princess and her lover were banished by the heavenly emperor, her father, to live on opposite sides of the Milky Way. Once a year, on the seventh night of the seventh month, a flock of magpies forms a bridge so that they may meet. However, if it should happen to rain, the magpies are said to be unable to do this so that the couple must wait for another year. To avoid such a sad fate as befell the weaver and the cowherd, children demonstrate their industry each year by writing out some calligraphy. Bamboo branches are erected in homes, nurseries and kindergartens, and decorated with wishes written out on tiny strips of coloured paper. Many of the inter-viewees reported that they celebrate this festival each year for their young children, and in Kurotsuchi it is the pupils who have just started school who are particularly honoured.

The chrysanthemum festival is no longer held on 9 September, but it seems to be quite popular to take children out on the evening of the full moon at about this time, and some families make a kind of rice cake to celebrate the occasion. Another annual occasion, celebrated particularly in families with children, is Christmas, again borrowed from the West, when cream cake is made, and department stores sell a variety of gifts and decorations. Some stores even engage a Santa Claus to deliver gifts to children at their homes.

Religious activities

Children of all ages also take an active part in the many festivals which are held throughout Japan, particularly in the summer months. These are usually associated with Shinto shrines, and take different forms in different parts of the country, but a common feature found in many of them is a procession of young children combining their forces to pull a portable shrine around the appro-priate district by means of a very long rope. Typically, members of the Youth Group, whose ages vary from fifteen to late thirties, supervise the children and help them to guide the shrine safely round corners, but this spectacular part of any festival is often dominated by the youngsters. In Tateyama the huge shrines had space inside them to carry drummers and flautists, roles again played by children, who practised their skills for weeks beforehand, filling the evening air with the exciting rhythms of the festival. Those who pull on the rope also join in from time to time with equally rhythmical shouts. School children play the most active part on such occasions, but the tiniest toddlers are encouraged to take a token place holding the rope, and mothers walk alongside them with babies on their backs. Special, brightly coloured jackets are worn by the participants, who also express their local allegiances by means of a coloured headband which is different for each district taking part. Larger festivals have activities for participants of all ages, but some smaller ones may be carried out almost entirely by children, with local men and perhaps members of the Youth Group organising and supervising the event.

Shinto shrines also sell charms and amulets for particular purposes, including occasions in the life cycle mentioned already, such as the 7–5–3 celebration and the baby's first visit. A charm may be purchased for the safe delivery of a baby, and a rite held to 'cure' an especially naughty child. At some shrines special gifts are prepared for the young visitors to festivals: one was a card game which comprised an alphabetical set of phrases and sayings encapsulating famous national events, festivals and important details of early training 'to nourish the shoots of a correct and beautiful heart and pass on to children the rich tradition of Japan'.[67] They included details about Shinto shrines and festivals, but also about behaviour appropriate for young children, such as 'answer clearly and cheerfully' and 'fold up clothes neatly'. Clearly the Shinto religion sees itself as having a role to play in the upbringing of its young parishioners.

Buddhism is in a common view in Japan more often associated with funerals and memorials for the dead than with the early part of life, but an event organised to celebrate the reconstruction of a historic building in a Buddhist temple in Tateyama included a procession of very small children, prepared for some two hours beforehand in the elaborate costumes they were to wear. The priest explained that children take part because of their purity and innocence, appropriate at this ceremony to give a soul to the new building. For the children's part, their parents hope that they will grow up good and happy by taking part in such a rare and auspicious event. Their mothers considered that their children had been lucky to be at the appropriate age when the building was finished.

Japanese Buddhism has also adopted a popular boddhisattva as a patron for small children. Jizō, or Kshitigarbha, known as an especially merciful boddhisattva who delivers souls from hell and helps people in their last moments before death, is also popular in China. It is only in Japan, however, that he has become associated with children, sometimes appearing as a boy or child himself in dreams described in stories about him, and apparently being especially concerned with the souls of children who die before hearing the teachings of Buddha. All over the country, stone and wooden images of Jizō are adorned with colourful bibs and little hats, offered to him by adults, many of whom may be praying for a child, perhaps a simple prayer, that a child should stop wetting his bed, or sleep better at night. An author who has published some stories in English about Jizō suggests that skilful propagators and preachers chose the form of a child for Jizō to popularise his cult 'for the hearts of the people, known for their love of children, were touched by the introduction of this frail, helpless and mysterious being'.[68]

Notes

1   Kenkyūsha's *New Japanese–English Dictionary* 1954.
2   Hara & Wagatsuma 1974: 1.
3   *Nihon Minzokugaku Jiten (Japan Folklore Dictionary)* 1979.
4   Hara & Wagatsuma 1974: 2.
5   E.g. Benedict 1977: 180; Smith 1962: 194.
6   *Pre-school Education in Japan* 1981: 9. Official translation.
7   *Early Childhood Education* 1979: 105. Translated by H. Kodama.
8   Deasey 1978: 37.
9   Hara & Wagatsuma 1974: 2–3.
10   Makino *et al.* 1970: 141.
11   Aoi 1976: 59.
12   E.g. Musashi 1982.
13   Hendry 1981: 114–16.
14   *Ibid.* 15ff; a recent 'rethinking' of recruitment strategies for household succession is to be found in Bachnik 1983.
15   *Ibid.* 100; cf. Inoguchi 1962: 224.
16   Suzuki Takao 1978A: 189–91; 1978B: 136–7.

17   See, for example, *Kōseihakusho* (*Ministry of Welfare White Paper*) 1979: 34.
18   Smith T. C. 1977: 11 & 63–4; Inoguchi 1962: 197; Hara & Wagatsuma 1974: 16.
19   Hara & Wagatsuma 1974: 11–15; Inoguchi 1962: 217, 224–5; c.f. Lebra T. S. 1976: 144. A similar idea is described by Leis (1963: 48) for the Ijaw.
20   Hara & Wagatsuma 1974: 13–14.
21   See, for example, Wolfenstein 1955: 169 and Newson 1977: 66–8 for a nineteenth-century religious view.
22   Hara & Wagatsuma 1974: 13; Inoguchi 1962: 216; in fact there has been some considerable discussion at an intellectual level about whether a child is born good, bad or as a 'white sheet', summarised from a historical point of view in Kojima 1983: 192–7.
23   Benedict 1977: 187.
24   Picone 1981: 26.
25   Benedict 1977: 187; Norbeck & Norbeck 1956: 660; Lock 1980: 173–5.
26   Deasey 1978: 37.
27   Ibuka 1976: 1; this book has apparently been translated into English and published by Souvenir Press, London.
28   *Ibid.* Inoguchi (1962: 218) suggests that while a child retains certain aspects of the character with which it is born, those inculcated through training and environment are dominant.
29   Connor 1977: 305ff.
30   Doi 1973: 82–3.
31   *Ibid.* 58.
32   *Ibid.* 83.
33   Cf. Shigaki 1983: 20 who describes this custom even in day nurseries.
34   Hendry 1981: 89; Smith and Schooler (1978) note the emphasis on the maternal role over the conjugal role.
35   From the household information provided by parents of children entering Shirayuri kindergarten, the following figures were obtained: out of a total of 176 children, 37 slept regularly in the same bedding as their mothers, 118 slept in the same room, and only 20 in separate rooms. One child slept with a grandmother. These figures may not be entirely representative as this private kindergarten necessarily draws on a high-income group, but the interview material seems to support the general trend, also noted by Caudill & Plath 1966: 344–66 and Befu 1971: 154–5.
36   Hara & Wagatsuma 1974: 38–9; Inoguchi 1962: 214–15; Norbeck & Devos in Hsu 1961 discussed Japanese work on the *ejiko* and its possible psychological effects.
37   Toilet training is one of the subjects which fascinated the culture–personality school, and diverse interpretations of the Japanese material fuelled their conflicts (see Norbeck & Devos 1961: 28). The discussion

here and in later chapters should illustrate the difference between the
social anthropological approach and that of the psychologically orientated observer who might attempt to draw conclusions about the
Japanese personality from such practices (e.g. Gorer 1962: 308–24 and
Labarre 1962: 334–59).

38 *Early Childhood Education* 1979: 63.
39 31 May 1981.
40 Kimura 1981: 119; children first learn *kana,* some ninety relatively
simple characters, which represent phonetic sounds. Stories and other
early reading matter are written entirely in this script.
41 Hara & Wagatsuma 1974: 15, 192.
42 Hendry 1981: 202; cf. Inoguchi 1962: 195.
43 Hara & Wagatsuma 1974: 19; cf. Yoda 1977: 5.
44 Fukutake 1976: 108.
45 Makino *et al.* 1970: 142. The particular changes from continuing to
nuclear family are discussed in Fukutake 1976: 98–109.
46 *Women and Education in Japan* 1980: 20.
47 Details of the government child welfare services are published in
English in a booklet entitled *A Brief Report on Child Welfare Services
in Japan* 1979, which also summarises the historical developments in
this field.
48 *Ibid.* 10.
49 *Early Childhood Education* 1979: 19.
50 *Ibid.* 98, 101; *Statistical Handbook of Japan* 1984: 123.
51 *A Brief Report of Child Welfare Services* 1979: 16.
52 Cf. *Early Childhood Education* 1979: 57.
53 *Rōdōkijunhō* (*Labour Standards Law*) Nos. 65 and 66.
54 E.g. Dore 1973: 33–4; Clark 1979: 118; van Helvoort 1979: 40.
55 *Pre-School Education in Japan* 1981: 19; *Statistical Handbook of
Japan* 1984: 130.
56 *Natsu no Seikatsu* (*Summer Life*). According to one informant, similar
books are distributed to primary school children and include spaces to
record teeth-cleaning, resolutions, holiday work, and even bowel
movements.
57 Stockwin 1982; 237–8. I am indebted to Brian Powell and Graham
Healey for bringing this to my attention.
58 *A Brief Report on Child Welfare Services* 1979: 11.
59 Hara & Wagatsuma 1974: 12–13.
60 Sofue 1965: 148–64 is a discussion of such variations in English, but
more detail may be found in Japanese in Hara & Wagatsuma 1974:
20–31, and e.g. Inoguchi 1962. I have also consulted a number of other
writers who mention specific ceremonies and these include Bacon
1891: 3; Smith R. J. 1962: 189–91; Maretzki & Maretzki 1963: 93,
104–5; von Siebold 1841: 172–6; Mitford 1966: 421–6; and Casal
1967. Further references may also be found in my own previous
discussion of these ceremonies (Hendry 1981: 200–6). For a nationally

accepted view, I have used works in Japanese such as Shiotsuki 1970 and 1971; and the *Nihon Minzokugaku Jiten* (*Japan Folklore Dictionary*) 1979.
61 Cf. Hara 1980– 2.
62 See, for example, Yokoe 1970: 176; von Siebold 1841: 175–6; Wakamori 1973: 295; Norbeck 1954: 157; *Nihon Minzokugaku Jiten* 1979: 315–16; Mitford 1966: 423–4.
63 Cf. Dore 1971: 248–9.
64 See, for example, Turner 1969; the Association of Social Anthropologists' Monograph on socialisation has four papers on youth and adolescents and only three on child training (Mayer 1970).
65 Yanagida 1957: 260.
66 Inouye 1910: 300.
67 Michael Pye brought this game to my attention and I am indebted to him for the translation of the section of the accompanying notes quoted here.
68 Dykstra 1978: 189, complete article 179–200. See also Inoguchi 1962: 217.

Chapter Two

The arenas and agents of socialisation

Socialisation of pre-school children in Japan is carried out in three main arenas, whose relative importance ideally changes as a child passes through three generally perceived stages of development. The three arenas are the home, the neighbourhood and the kindergarten or day nursery, each of which will be considered in a separate section of this chapter. The three stages are distinguished mainly by vocabulary and attitudes. The first is separated linguistically from the other two as the 'suckling period' (*nyūjiki*), approximately the first year of a child's life, after which the pre-school years are taken together as *yōjiki*. The division of the second stage is based on collective ideas that a child of three begins to respond to reason and will therefore 'listen' to its caretakers, so that the approach to rearing may develop from the first 'creation' of the soul, implied in the saying 'the soul of the three-year-old lasts till 100'.

The home is of course important throughout a child's life, but the view is often expressed that a baby or 'suckling' should be moved as little as possible from the immediate environment of its family and their abode. A forcible illustration of this idea arose when my assistant's baby ran a temperature during a couple of nights away from home. On her return, she became adamant that the baby should not be moved again. Her own mother chastised her for taking the baby away, arguing that taking it out amongst people lowers its resistance to germs, excites it, breaks up its routines and rhythms, and could well cause the baby to wake up and cry during the night. Other informants reinforced this view in reference to self-imposed limitations on their usual activities during the first year of a baby's life. Even a mother with employment outside the home tries to entrust a baby to the care of a relative or close neighbour during this early stage, and it is reported that only 1.7 per cent of all babies under one

year are taken to day nurseries or other such facilities. Seventy-one
per cent of working women's children under one year are cared for in
their own homes, probably usually by a grandparent, and fourteen
per cent in other homes, so that most are in the charge of individuals.[1] The general disapproval of 'baby hotels' is indicative of the
collective idea that home is the more appropriate environment.

As the infant learns to walk, it begins to venture out into the
neighbourhood, at first accompanied by a caretaker, but as it
approaches the age of three it may be allowed to play with other
children if the area close to the home is considered sufficiently safe.
In Kurotsuchi toddlers are often to be seen playing in the shrine
compound, their caretakers nearby but not necessarily interfering
with the activities of the children on the swings and slides supplied
there, as long as they are in no danger. The view is often expressed
that this is the stage when children should start to make friends with
other infants of their own age, and in a booklet published by the
Chiba prefectural department of education to help mothers of children in the *yōji* stage, it is said to be necessary (*hitsuyō*) from the age of
two for children to start playing with other children in the neighbourhood.[2] At this time, the agents of socialisation increase in
number as the caretakers of other toddlers enter the scene, and the
child begins to learn about its relations with peers. Older children
also become important, but inter-relationships are still informal and
the child can usually retreat to its home territory if it becomes
overwhelmed.

During its fourth or fifth year usually, although this may be earlier,
a child will enter a local kindergarten or day nursery, where it comes
into contact with institutionalised socialisation under the guidance
of professional caretakers, although, again, other children may be as
much involved in the process as adults are. This is the period also
when a child may be enrolled in private classes for particular accomplishments. Now the child is fully entered into the third stage in
pre-school development and all three arenas have come into play. In
the following pages some detail of each stage will be provided,
together with a discussion of recent changes.

The home

The composition of the household in which a child spends its early years varies depending on the family circumstances. Nuclear families, which have become increasingly common in modern Japan, are similar to those found in the West. The archetypal parents-and-two-children unit is in fact by far the most common,[3] the two children frequently being born within the space of two or three years, so that large numbers of siblings, common within living memory as important influences in growing up, are now relatively rare. The continuing family, which is the other still common type of domestic arrangement, almost always involves only one conjugal pair in each generation. Thus, the child growing up in such a family is in close contact with one set of grandparents and possibly one or two great grandparents, as well as its parents, but cousins and married uncles and aunts usually live elsewhere. Unmarried siblings of the parent whose natal home it is may be present for a period, and have a right to stay in the house if they never marry.

In the areas where research was carried out there were both types of family. In Kurotsuchi, a rural community with a large number of farmers, most of the houses were old family lines, so the vast majority were continuing families. Even those who had set up new homes, since only one son in a continuing family remains in the ancestral home, had proceeded in the next generation to bring in a spouse and continue in the traditional way. In Tateyama there was more variety. Details were available in some of the kindergartens where family information was kept, although if a child came from a two-generation household it was impossible to tell from the records whether it was a new nuclear family or a continuing one where the grandparents had died. One of the areas in which I worked was quite rural with a situation similar to Kurotsuchi. Of the 113 children in the local kindergarten, 99 lived in continuing families and 14 in nuclear ones. At Shirayuri Kindergarten, the only private one and therefore representing the better-off of Tateyama, 82 of the pupils lived in continuing families and 98 in nuclear ones. At Tateyama Kindergarten, one of the central public ones in the city, 121 children lived in continuing ones and 252 in nuclear ones. In all these examples, some of the 'nuclear' figures are probably continuing families with only two generations alive. Of the 49 families I interviewed for this investigation, 28 lived with senior parents and 21 in nuclear families, but in this case I know that all the nuclear families are also new families. The Kyushu families in the sample had 18 to four in favour of the continuing line, whereas the Tateyama and Tokyo ones included only 10 continuing families and 17 nuclear ones.

In either type of family, where geographically possible, other close relatives are likely to be frequent visitors and since these seem to be regarded as appropriate people to admonish and teach a child, they may well play quite an important part in their early rearing. Grandparents, in particular, are usually involved, ritually if not practically, and if they live too far for frequent contact, children often spend a week or longer periods in their home during the kindergarten holidays.

Thus, the categories of human being that a child first learns to distinguish are the parents, grandparents, uncles, aunts and cousins, much as may be the case in Western society. The terminology, too, does not differ greatly. Even where the continuing family is the residential unit, the terms for grandfather and grandmother are the same for both sets of couples, that for the non-resident pair being qualified with a plàce-name or some other distinguishing feature. No distinction is made between maternal and paternal uncles, aunts and cousins, and second cousins are not usually distinguished terminologically from first cousins. The chief difference between this system and the Western one is that older and younger siblings are distinguished so that there are separate words for elder brother and younger brother, elder sister and younger sister, which introduces an element of hierarchy into the sibling relationship.

All terms of relationship are expressed from the point of view of the youngest member. Thus the terms for grandmother and grandfather are applied by everyone to the oldest generation, even by their own children once they have become parents. As new babies are born, their elder siblings are addressed more and more as 'elder brother' and 'elder sister', rather than by their first names. In principle, seniors address juniors by their first names and juniors use a relationship term for their superiors but the relationship terms are used to children to encourage them to behave in a grown-up manner.

Within this group of close family, then, how are the child-rearing responsibilities distributed? It seems to be the common view nowadays that the ultimate responsibility for a child rests with the mother, whether the domestic arrangements involve three generations or not.[4] From a Western point of view, this may seem to be quite natural, but in a traditional household (*ie*) the children were regarded as belonging to the house, whether the mother was present or not. Thus, if a girl had a baby out of wedlock and subsequently married, the child would often stay in the mother's natal home; or if a woman left a house on divorce or separation, it was usual for the children to remain behind, to be brought up by the new wife or their grandmother. For example, one of my informants in Kurotsuchi lived with his wife and his father's second wife, his own mother having been divorced from his father when he was a baby and now she was living in Hawaii. His young brother, the uterine son of the second wife, had left the house on marriage, since he was not the eldest son, who is preferred to inherit in the system of primogeniture usually practised. In the past, a common reason for divorce was said to be when the wife failed to get on with her mother-in-law, even if relations with her husband were quite reasonable, but nowadays it seems to be more likely in such circumstances for the young couple to leave the family home, taking their children with them. The legal registration system, which now records each nuclear family as a separate unit, also supports this practice. In case of divorce, it is getting more and more likely that children will remain with their mother.[5]

Evidence for the attitude that the mother bears the ultimate responsibility for her children was provided during research in several ways. For example, where grandmothers taking charge of small children while their mothers were out at work were interviewed about their child-rearing practices, they usually commented that it should really be the mother who answered the questions as they were just standing in. In some cases, grandmothers received pocket money from their daughters or daughters-in-law who were out at work as specific remuneration for child care. When one grandmother was invited to go on a trip with her age-mates, her daughter-in-law was expected to take time off work so that she could go.

Nevertheless, within specific families, mothers often reported that in a difference between mother and grandmother over a matter of child-rearing, the grandmother would still usually be deferred to. When I reported to a PTA group that in England our mothers advise us, but that in the end we English mothers tend to go our own way, the audience responded with gasps of surprise. It has been reported from survey material that many parents prefer to rely on the advice of their own mothers, or their own experience from childhood, than to follow the advice of modern magazines and 'scientific' recommendations.[6] The figures are higher for rural areas than urban ones, but in studies carried out in Nagoya and Okayama cities, these were still around fifty per cent of respondents.[7] However, mothers frequently complain that grandmothers do too much for a child so that it fails to learn to do things for itself. They also say that grandparents are too lenient with children, giving them anything they ask for and cancelling punishments meted out by parents. Grandparents are also said to emphasise too often the dangers surrounding the child, thus making it too cautious and unadventurous, though the caretakers defend themselves by pointing out that they must be especially careful with children who are not their own. Grandfathers are often not distinguished from grandmothers in these comments, each apparently as likely to indulge a child as the other. Indeed, in Kurotsuchi, it seemed more often the grandfather who was the culprit in such accusations. It was certainly often the grandfather who spent a large part of the day with the child.

It is evident that these conflicts will arise less in nuclear families where the grandparents are only visitors to the home, but there are many working mothers in nuclear families who live near enough to relatives to take advantage of their offers to take care of children from an early age, so that these cases provide a wider range of agents of socialisation in the early period. This was the case in five out of seventeen nuclear families in the Tateyama interview sample. One such family provided an interesting case in this respect. It was a nuclear family in which the mother had a full-time job, but her elder sister, whose husband had moved into and agreed to inherit the family home, was barren. Thus, the elder sister took care of the children in the early period and arranged all their childhood ceremonies in the family home. In exchange, she hoped that the younger sister, whom she had formally adopted to inherit the home when she died, would thereby furnish the house (*ie*) with a male heir in the form of her son. In this case an aunt has taken on an important role in the socialisation of the child, along the lines of the traditional ideology of the house, as discussed in Chapter 1.

The benefits of having an heir to continue the family line include the provision of someone to take responsibility for the older members in their declining years, as well as to carry out ancestral memorials after they die. Thus usually grandparents, though in the last case the aunt, have a vested interest in contributing to the socialisation of the younger generation of their family line. Many nuclear families have ultimately to bear the responsibility of caring for their elderly parents and ancestors even if they are not currently co-resident. Thus it seems appropriate for small children to spend time staying with their grandparents even if they live long distances away. Another nuclear family in the sample sends a son each summer to spend several weeks in the mother's home village, where he is accepted as a member of the community. In this case the mother's family has a son who plans to inherit the family home, but the country community is thought to be good experience for the child in the summer holidays. The mother's mother is also sometimes preferred as a caretaker when a mother-in-law is not keen on the task, or when the mother's relations with her are not good.

In neither the nuclear nor the continuing family does the father usually play a very active part in the early child-rearing process. Recently there has been some publicity given to the way fathers have begun to become more involved with their babies in Western societies, particularly from a feminist element of Japanese society,[8] and it is said to be good for a father to have as much contact as possible with his children. Indeed, in some families these principles are put into practice and fathers are even helping with feeding and changing of their babies.[9] In general, however, fathers express great interest in child-rearing at a theoretical level, some claiming to have as much contact as possible with their children, but the majority of my female informants report that the father is in practice little involved. In many cases the pressure of work prevents the father being present much in the family home, many men returning home each evening after their children are asleep, and leaving in the morning before they get up. It is sometimes emphasised that the father's work comes first, even in family businesses where he is actually on the premises all day. Two such wives in the interview sample complained that their husbands spend very little time with the children. Other wives seemed quite resigned to the fact that their husbands spend most of their evenings drinking with their colleagues.

In response to a question put to the families in the interview sample about the role of the father in child-rearing, many families reported that it was he who bathed the child(ren) if he was home in time. It should perhaps be pointed out that the Japanese bath is something of an institution, a relaxing, pleasurable activity, rather than merely being a means to become clean. In most families the children bathe with their parents and grandparents of both sexes until they are quite grown up, and the bath is seen as a good place to be together and discuss the events of the day. The sting in the tail for the mother, where very small children are concerned, is that she must wait outside the bathroom where all the fun is taking place, so that she can dry and dress the children when they come out. But at least it is easier for her to do this than it is for her to dry herself and the babies at the same time if there is no other adult to help. The bath is too deep and too hot to sit babies in by themselves. In continuing families it is often a grandparent who will help out by bathing the children. According to the Norbecks, the baby was often bathed by the father because they shared the privilege of being allowed first in the clean, hot water.[10]

Several families also reported that the father sometimes found time on Sundays to take out his child(ren) or play with them, but this kind of activity tends to increase as the child gets older. In families with a new baby it seems to be regarded as a father's role to help more with the older child. In public places, such as parks and other amusements visited by young families, it is possible to observe this principle in practice, although it is not unusual these days to see a father carrying a baby or pushing round a push-chair. Most fathers seem to draw the line at strapping babies to their backs, however, and when I reported at a PTA meeting at Shirayuri Kindergarten that back-carriers for babies are often carried by men in England, the response was gales of laughter. In Kurotsuchi it was not an uncommon sight to see a grandfather with a baby on his back, and it has been reported that boys used to do it in the past,[11] so perhaps it is just unseemly for fathers, rather than for males in general.

Some mothers reported that it was up to the father to get cross or be strict with the children, but this was more often the case in families with school-age children, and one mother in particular said that her older sons were too big for her to discipline effectively. The Maretzkis reported that in Okinawa the father may be called upon as a 'last resort threat', but he was not often involved with child-rearing,[12] while Singer wrote of mainland Japan specifically that the father was 'not called upon as a last reserve of sternness and punitive power'.[13] The Maretzkis also comment that the father's presence in the home affects the children's behaviour,[14] and one of the mothers in the interview sample said that her son never misbehaves when her husband is at home. In the past it was expected that the father would preserve a dignified, rather distant role, confirmed by the mother's teaching that the father should be respected, but in nuclear families it seems to be more common nowadays for the father to adopt a more friendly attitude.[15]

Individual families in the interview sample report activities between father and child such as reading together, taking to kindergarten on Saturday, consoling and changing in the night, taking to the toilet first thing in morning, washing hands and cleaning teeth, and putting to bed when the mother is out or unwell. A song taught to the children at Shirayuri Kindergarten, to be sung at the sports day when many fathers are present, encouraged the youngsters almost to worship their fathers:

Papa, papa, erai erai papa	Dad, dad, great great Dad,
Sekai no dareyori erainda	He's the greatest in the world
Ookina okuchi de warattara	If he laughs with his big mouth
Kaijū mitai ni mieru kedo	He looks like a monster, but . . .
Sutekina, sutekina papa nanda	He's a wonderful, wonderful Dad.
Papa, papa, tsuyoi tsuyoi papa	Dad, dad, strong, strong dad
Sekai no dare yori tsuyoinda	He's the strongest in the world
Okotta okao wa kowai kedo	His cross face is frightening but
Hontō wa tottemo yasashikute	He's really very kind, and
Sutekina, sutekina papa nanda	He's a wonderful, wonderful Dad.

It could be said that it was in the interest of a private kindergarten to sweeten the people who pay the fees, and great efforts were made to amuse them at sports day, but at a special evening occasion arranged for fathers to discuss their children's progress with the teachers, only twenty-one out of a possible 170 or so accepted the invitation.

An older sibling is usually encouraged to participate in the socialisation of the younger one and great emphasis is laid on the status of 'elder brother' or 'elder sister'. This seems to be a successful ploy in many families to avoid jealousy when a new baby is born. The older child is usually encouraged to help and give way to the younger one, and much play is made of the fact that being older one is therefore more experienced and able 'to understand'. A definite superior role is being outlined for the older child, who seems to take great pride in playing it. This places an interesting early emphasis on the concept of hierarchy, since it is the benevolence and responsibility of the superior role which is being encouraged.

The distinction between younger and older brother and sister is also emphasised in a use of language encouraged. Older children 'do things for' a younger child (*naninani o shite ageru*), whereas this phrase is discouraged if used by a younger child to an older one. For example, in the case of the verb to play, the older child does the younger child the favour of playing with it (*asonde ageru*), but in the reverse situation, where it wanted to play with a still older child, it would have to make the suggestion in the form of a request which implies a degree of deference (*asonde kureru*). This introduces the other, inferior side of hierarchial relations and corresponds to speech forms used in polite conversation when one humbles oneself in order to show respect to another. Children are not expected to master these general niceties very early, but the presence of the grandparents is sometimes cited as an opportunity for mothers to encourge them to begin to use simple forms of respect language.

Nowadays no discussion of the agents of socialisation in the home would be complete without mention of the television set. Few families are without one, there are numerous channels to choose from, and morning television abounds with programmes for pre-school children and their mothers. Many of these shows present quite explicit child-training material, reinforcing the teachings of mothers throughout Japan. Some of the detail will be mentioned in subsequent chapters, but the form resembles that of *Sesame Street*, with large, speaking animal-like characters who blunder about behaving in the wrong way so that they can be corrected by a gentle, friendly (sometimes male) mother-figure who explains to them the proper way to proceed. The important points are reinforced in songs and ditties, often sung by children, and a plethora of other devices designed to appeal to and remain in the minds of tiny viewers. Characters of Japanese writing are also featured in an early programme, supporting the mothers' claim that their children learn to read through television.

This adds a public dimension to socialisation, even in the home, which is of course evident too in the books and pamphlets distributed to mothers of babies and young children. Television programmes supplement this literature so that mothers, too, may be socialised in the appropriate way to socialise their children. Since many of these broadcasts and publications are initiated on a national level, even if they are actually put out by the prefectural or municipal authorities, they are probably a strong force for homogeneity in approach throughout the country. Regional variations in child-rearing practices undoubtedly still exist, but it seems likely that they are diminishing in force and number. Although many mothers in the survey mentioned above reported that they followed their own mothers rather than the new 'scientific' methods advised in books and magazines, a number of grandmothers discussed the ways in which they had modified their own rearing methods in the light of modern advice. Details of changes in practice will be discussed in subsequent chapters.

The neighbourhood

In many parts of Japan, there is an institutional aspect to neighbourhood relations. Communities may be divided up into fixed groups which share various responsibilities for public property, and, within the groups, members of the houses involved have fixed roles at certain important times for each of the other houses.[16] Typically, neighbours will participate in each other's weddings, births and deaths, as well as perhaps attending the ceremonies associated with the growing up of each other's children. Even where such groups are not formally created, informal aid is usually given between houses popularly delineated as 'the three opposite and one on either side' (*mukōsangen ryōdonari*), although the actual participation in such co-operative activity may not of course be distributed exactly in this way. In cities, where the population of neighbourhoods may be more fluid than in the country, it is the custom for a family moving in to take a small gift to the near neighbours as a convenient way of introducing themselves and expressing a willingness to co-operate in local activities. Even in a housing estate near Chiba, where one of the interviewees had recently built a house and all the neighbours were in houses constructed in the last few years, the families had already organised several local co-operative groups.

Thus, it is common in Japan for a family to be acquainted with other families living nearby, and for its members to know and co-operate with their counterparts in neighbouring houses. In particular, in this context, mothers of young children meet at the local swings, discuss their problems with each other, and occasionally look after each other's children when the need arises. For the children themselves, these neighbours are probably the first representatives of the world outside the family circle with whom they have repeated contact, and their children may well be their first friends.

Close neighbours may in fact be classified in familial terms, so that other mothers become 'aunts', fathers become 'uncles', and their children become 'big brothers' and 'big sisters', according to their ages. Older children refer to younger ones by their given names, with a diminutive suffix '*chan*', just as is the case within the family. For clarity, the given names or surnames of the individuals concerned may be appended, as may a place or occupational name such as 'the aunt from the corner shop' or 'next door's big brother' and so on. Again, a hierarchical element is present, now perhaps better recognised, as children are explicitly encouraged to be polite to the adults, show a degree of respect for the older children, and help and care for the younger ones. There is again a role for the older ones to teach the younger ones and be benevolent to them when disputes arise: indeed, one of my informants commented that a neighbour's daughter was more efficient than she at socialising her daughter. As we met neighbours in the areas where we stayed, the relative ages of our children was always one of the first matters to be sorted out so that the appropriate terms could be used, and the appropriate behaviour encouraged.

Perhaps as important as the hierarchical element, however, it is thought to be necessary at this stage for children to learn to play happily with any other children who happen to be there. This is the beginning of social life, the creation of the social being, and a child who is unsuccessful playing with the children in the neighbourhood is thought likely to have trouble in its future social relations. On the household information sheet filled out on entry at kindergartens there is often a space to enter the child's good points in the view of the parents. A point quite frequently mentioned was the child's ability to play with anyone, and if the child had difficulty in this respect, it might be entered in the section for bad points, or points to be rectified. Since any one neighbourhood usually has a number of children of different ages, the existence of some accepted ideas about hierarchy seems to aid the likelihood of harmony amongst the children.

Less emphasis is placed at this stage on sex, and indeed, lists of friends of children entering Shirayuri Kindergarten included several examples of children of different sexes as particularly good friends at that time. Later, single-sex groups become common, but in the early stages boys and girls seem to get on well. One family in the interview sample teased a daughter now in university about the fact that her closest playmate before school had been a little boy. Although they still lived near to the boy's family, she had had little to do with him after starting school and was surprised to find out that he had been so close.

Thus little gangs of children of both sexes may be seen roaming about in many parts of Japan from quite an early age. In the country they will play in the fields, or on the footpaths which crisscross the villages; in cities they will play in quiet back-streets or parks; even apartment buildings often have an open space at one side, or a courtyard in the middle, where children may play. At first mothers may supervise their toddlers as they venture out into this social world, but gradually they will leave them to trail after the bigger children, learning the rules as they go. When sibling groups were larger, five-year-olds were entrusted with the care of babies, but this is rarely observed these days.

Such activities are rather informal for pre-school children, serving mainly to introduce them to a social world outside their own home and circle of relatives. Some older children may act as important agents of socialisation, reinforcing the teaching of mothers and other caretakers if they take seriously their role of older brother or sister. For others, it may just be a convenient way to learn ball games, and how to catch and keep the insects which abound in the summer. In the past, however, this neighbourhood play was seen as an important part of a child's education, and some adults lament the fact that kindergarten and other classes have severely reduced the number of hours children have available for such play. As long ago as the early part of this century, Yanagita Kunio, an influential Japanese folklorist, questioned the value of the middle-class preference to keep their children in, and the separation in kindergarten of children of different ages into groups supervised by adults. He pointed out that as children of different ages played together outside they gradually learned the ideas of equality and justice – important steps on the way to an independent life.[17] Smaller sibling groups and the extension of the kindergartens and day nurseries to include all social classes are factors which have further reduced such experience. Outside play continues, but apparently on a greatly reduced scale to that of the past ,[18] when the local community was more involved generally in the rearing of its children.

A still flourishing element of many neighbourhoods begins on a more organised basis when children enter school and qualify to join a children's group (*kodomogumi*). These are based on local residential units and the children thus express a formal allegiance with the neighbourhood by joining them. Traditionally these groups were active in villages, especially for festivals and other religious activities, but many fell into decline as industrialisation proceeded.[19] Recently they have been revived in many areas, organising sporting activities, outings and school disciplinary groups as well as participating in festivals and other ceremonies in the old way. In neighbourhoods in

Tokyo, as well as in country villages such as Kurotsuchi, children of a neighbourhood gather at a meeting point every morning in order to walk to school together. Thus, the relations established informally at an early age are likely to continue, and even for children whose families move, there are similar groups for them to join in other areas.

Kindergartens, day nurseries and other classes

Most children in Japan today experience the third arena of institutionalised socialisation before they enter compulsory education in their seventh year. In 1981, 65.7 per cent of all children of the appropriate age had enrolled in a kindergarten,[20] and most of the rest attend day nurseries, either because the longer hours are convenient for their working mothers, or because day nurseries are more readily available in areas where most mothers do in fact work. These institutions have come to replace part of the element of public socialisation previously assigned rather informally to the community, and about forty per cent of all kindergartens and sixty per cent of day nurseries are publicly owned.[21] The private institutions have to meet national minimum standards, set by the Ministry of Education for kindergartens and the Ministry of Health and Welfare for day nurseries, although the purpose of early childhood education is considered to be the same in both types of institution.[22]

It is usually emphasised that they aim to supplement home education, 'to develop the minds and health of the children', and to introduce them to group life in preparation for entry into primary school. In the case of day nurseries, they have the additional purpose of helping families who are unable to provide full care for their children, initially because economic circumstances made it necessary for both parents to work, but, more recently, 'to enable . . . parents to enjoy culturally rich lives, mothers to work in areas best suited to their abilities, and to take part in social activities'.[23]

The first kindergarten was established in 1876 at the Tokyo Women's Normal School and it still operates there in what is now known as Ochanomizu Women's University. It was organised along Froebelian lines and its pupils were mainly from upper-class families. It is still a very prestigious institution, regarded as 'progressive' in its approach, which nowadays resembles that of an English kindergarten much more than do the methods of most Japanese ones. After this, kindergartens began to open in other parts of the country, often established by Christian organisations, but it was only after the Second World War that their number increased dramatically, and only in the last few years that kindergarten education has become available to almost any family who wants it.[24]

The kindergartens have been subjected to various ideological movements since their inception, reflecting those of Europe and the United States, but nowadays still retain a discernable Froebelian influence. In prewar Japan there was also a strong nationalistic emphasis which included 'group education' to replace 'free education', which had been adopted during the previous liberal period. Today's kindergartens seem to have synthesised these apparently opposing influences into a particularly Japanese combination which will be described in detail in Chapter five.[25]

Day nurseries were conceived as an idea during the early part of the nineteenth century, but only began to appear in fact at the end of the century when the industrial revolution created problems of child care in the new urban slums. At first they were established and operated by the people themselves, but gradually the Ministry of Home Affairs became involved in their organisation and funding. After the Rice Riots in 1918, public day nurseries were established, first in Osaka and then in other cities throughout Japan. Demand for female labour during the Second World War led to a greater need for nurseries, which were opened in Buddhist temples, Shinto shrines, libraries and schools. Since then their number has increased steadily and appears still to be rising.[26]

There is obviously some ideological variation between institutions run by religious bodies and those run by private individuals and government agencies. Some kindergartens have specific aims such as early musical training or the practice of Montessori methods. In large cities some kindergartens are attached to prestigious universities where there are also primary and secondary schools, so that children who gain a place in the kindergarten are thought to have a better chance eventually to gain a place in the university, and thereby secure for themselves a good job afterwards. Some such kindergartens have interviews for three-year-olds and choose the most promising, others prefer to assess their mothers. The nature of the education system, which theoretically provides any child with the possibility of upward social mobility, but makes it more likely if the child can gain admission to an academically-orientated school, has led to a demand for an early emphasis on intellectual activities. Private kindergartens all over Japan respond to this demand and there are small private classes after kindergarten for training in particular skills (*juku*). This 'over-intellectualistic' approach has been seen as a problem in Japanese kindergartens,[27] which are not expected by the Ministry of Education to provide training in academic skills such as reading and writing. There seems now to be an emphasis in some of the more 'progressive' private kindergartens on 'free play' as a speciality.

In the areas of my research it was in fact a small minority of parents who were very concerned at this early stage with sending their children to special kindergartens and academically orientated classes. There is often a choice, especially where parents can afford the private establishments, but factors such as convenience and children's friendships may be seen as more important than the ideology of the institution. Thus non-Christians may well outnumber Christians in kindergartens and nurseries attached to churches, and Shirayuri Kindergarten in Tateyama was often chosen for prestige, because it had a bus, or because it took children younger than the public establishments, rather than because it offered extra tuition in music and English. The headmistress there claimed never to turn away a child because it performed badly in the interview, but she admitted that she objected to mothers who were not well dressed for the occasion. In Yame, the city to which Kurotsuchi belongs, there are many more day nurseries than kindergartens, which suits the farming and other families whose adult members are all engaged in economically productive activities.

Once children enter a kindergarten or day nursery, they find themselves in a highly structured situation. Usually they are divided by age so that most of their contact with other children will be with peers, great emphasis being placed on the ideal that all the children should be friends (*tomodachi*) and get on well with one another. Best friends are not particularly encouraged, indeed there is not really such a concept at this stage, and a Japanese girl in England recently reeled off to me a whole list of 'best friends' she had made at her English school. Conflict and competition is discouraged, and each child is expected to participate equally in the many and varied communal activities. Duties are allocated to each member of the class each day, but every child has a turn eventually to serve and to discipline the others.

Much is made of the equality and sameness of the 'friends' surrounding one in an establishment such as this. Some have complete uniforms, little distinguishing one child from another, most have at least overalls and caps which are identical for boys and girls, except perhaps that their caps are different colours to indicate the classroom to which they belong. They have identical sets of equipment kept in identical drawers and shelves, although each child does at least have its own personal set, which is more than can be said of English kindergartens and nurseries where crayons, scissors and so forth are usually common property. In Tateyama, each child also has an emergency earthquake hood, again identical, and these are kept on hooks where the children also hang their bags, distinguished from each other only by their names and possibly little stickers, which give the children a chance to express their own identity. Thus, the child who has been much fussed over, and attended to night and day, now finds itself among perhaps thirty-nine other children,[28] each equally important in the eyes of the teacher, and each equally entitled to her attention.

This is not aimed to turn the children into little robots or automatons, as some Western observers like to see it, but to impress upon the child that the world is full of people just like itself whose needs and desires are equally important. Their names are known – the register is read out each day when each child must answer clearly – and their quirks and character differences become common knowledge as the children move through the classes and often into school together. Fun and enjoyment are perfectly possible in a kindergarten – indeed, they are among the aspects most stressed by teachers and parents alike, but they require co-operation and consideration, and the other members of the peer group become forceful agents of socialisation into this stage of development.

In most kindergartens and nurseries there is also some opportunity for older and younger children to interact, so that the 'elder brothers' and 'elder sisters' may still be encouraged to set an example to the younger ones, and perhaps take care of them in certain circumstances. At Shirayuri, for example, a new child will be assigned an older one to sit beside on the kindergarten bus, and the older one makes sure that the younger one learns the routine at going-home time. Almost every kindergarten and day nursery seems to have birthday parties from time to time, typically monthly to celebrate all the birthdays of that period at once, and on such an occasion all the children assemble together. Thus it is a good opportunity to point out the activities of the older ones as an example to the younger ones, which provides a responsibility for the former to consider in their singing or whatever activity happens to be the order of the day. If one of the top class should misbehave, it is suggested to them that one of the smaller children might see them and pick up bad behaviour, which would be quite inappropriate for big brothers and sisters. In some kindergartens, where numbers are limited, the children of two years' intake may be put together, which gives the teacher plenty of opportunity to use her older children to demonstrate to the younger ones the proper way to do things, again providing the older children with a responsible role and the younger ones with an example.

Of course, the teacher, too, now becomes an important person in the lives of the children. The head of Shirayuri Kindergarten encouraged her teachers to be crisp and efficient and to dress gaily but smartly to carry out the role which she saw as more important than that of a university teacher, since they have the children at such an impressionable age. They were kind with the children, but very firm, and crying was behaviour to be ignored rather than indulged. The benevolence of the teacher is for the children who put their energies into co-operating and participating enthusiastically in the many and varied activities she arranges for them. If she is a good teacher, she will show no favouritism, and most of her attention is directed to supervising the class as a body. The content of her (or occasionally his) instruction will form the subject matter of Chapter V.

In day nurseries there are smaller groups for smaller children, from one adult per three babies under one year, gradually increasing the number of children up to thirty per adult for four- and five-year-olds (see Chapter V for national standards). In the infants' classes the supervisors are nursery nurses, who have different training, and who aim to try and give their charges some of the love and attention they are perceived to lack at home. The older children may have a teacher who is trained for kindergarten, but she is often also a nursery nurse. Since the children usually spend the whole day in the establishment, they all take a nap in the afternoon, when a fair amount of patience and affectionate encouragement seems to be the best way to settle so many infants at the same time. The straight kindergarten teacher also needs a good measure of patience, and affection too, perhaps, but her image is somewhat different from the more motherly role of the nursery nurse.

Finally, some pre-school children begin to be influenced strongly by the teachers of private classes in particular skills. These are more commonly associated with older children preparing for entrance to academic secondary schools, but many classes are also available for primary school and kindergarten pupils. A typical selection open to pre-school children in a fairly densely populated area includes art, drawing, calligraphy, piano, violin, electric organ, ballet, rhythmics, Japanese dance, gymnastics, martial arts such as *kendō* and *aikidō*, swimming, football and more academic subjects such as English and Kumon-style mathematics. The nature of the classes is of course quite variable. Some are highly structured and especially sought by parents to provide an element of old fashioned discipline in their children's lives. Among these are *kendō*, where they may also learn the old samurai rules and ideology as a kind of sound philosophy for life; calligraphy, which emphasises the beauty of the Japanese script and the importance of writing it correctly; and Japanese dance, which is again concerned with very formalised and structured movement. An art or drawing class, on the other hand, may aim to develop some freedom of expression and a feeling for shape and colour in the young child. A chain of art schools throughout Japan base their teaching on a famous American school whose ideas are currently popular. The music classes may concentrate on Western classics, but some are very rigid in their teaching methods and discipline is again an important part of their training. The Suzuki violin schools have of course had a great impact in the West in the way they teach very young children to become accomplished musicians. Also popular are piano and electric organ classes. Sports of one sort or another seem to be becoming popular too for youngsters, and skating was a less common option open to pre-school children in Tateyama. The newest academic activity for children of the most ambitious parents seemed in 1981 to be the Kumon-style mathematics classes which aim to train pupils to respond almost automatically to mathematical problems.

The numbers of children who actually attend these classes may not always be very high at the kindergarten stage. From information supplied to the Tateyama public kindergarten when children entered the 1981 academic year, it was calculated that only twenty per cent of the five-to-six-year-olds and three per cent of the four-to-five-year-olds were actually registered in outside classes at that time. Numbers may well have increased during the year, of course. During the summer term of Shirayuri Kindergarten, where parents were more likely to be motivated to encourage their children's education since they had chosen a private kindergarten, the numbers of both four-to-five-year-olds and five-to-six-year-olds were nearer the forty per cent mark. Nearly twenty per cent of three-year-olds were involved too. In all cases there were more girls taking classes than boys, and many of these were only taking extra piano tuition at the kindergarten itself. The children of doctors seemed to be under particular pressure, especially to attend the more academically orientated classes such as 'Kumon', and some such children were involved in three different types of activity. In Kyushu there were no figures available from kindergartens, but only one of the interviewees had a pre-school child enrolled in a class, in this case for the electric organ. Information from a study carried out in kindergartens in the Tokyo area suggest much higher numbers of children attending classes there, with seventeen per cent of three-year-olds, 54 per cent of four-year-olds, and all the five-year-olds being involved in some kind of training of this sort, but no details were given of the kind of kindergartens at which the study was made. A survey carried out in Tokyo, Nagoya and Osaka came up with figures more resembling those of Tateyama with 39.2 per cent of children going to classes in accomplishments, and 2.4 per cent in study.[29]

Hara has pointed out that these classes, which may well operate at different times for different children in a neighbourhood, have removed the possibility of long continuous periods of time for play, particularly when children reach school age and more and more are enrolled for extra tuition of one sort or another. She goes on to add that nowadays children are less involved than they used to be in household chores, partly because of smaller families and the increased use of electric gadgets, but also in the interests of their studies, so there is still time for play, but it is fragmented. Thus, solitary pursuits, such as reading and watching television have come to replace activities with children in the neighbourhood. Instead, she goes on, more children are seeking peer group identity among friends who are attending the same tutoring classes, and those who don't attend are being deprived of the opportunity to form peer groups.[30]

This argument was supported by an informant who gave private English classes after school. He claimed that so many friendships are now formed in this way that children who don't attend such classes find themselves without friends, which adds an interesting group element to a phenomenon which must at first have started out to encourage individual achievement. However, another writer on the subject, who also comments on the element of friendship involved, points out that it provides a close interpersonal relationship between pupil and teacher which used to characterise Japanese learning, but which has been lost in recent mass education. Thus, she claims, special classes contain the seeds of 'a positive, progressive educational movement'.[31] Opal Dunn has suggested that for young children the teacher is often more like an 'elder sister' than a formal teacher. At Shirayuri Kindergarten, whose graduates are often dispersed to schools in their own residential areas when they leave, after-school classes in English and music provide excellent opportunities for kindergarten classmates to maintain their friendships throughout their school lives. A similar situation was described by the head of a kindergarten in Kyushu which also specialised in musical training, and continued classes for school children.

It seems to be the case, then, that these after-school classes have a socialising role apart from the obvious one connected with their content. This is likely to be more important for school children than for most younger children, except perhaps for those in some areas of Tokyo and other large cities. Thus, the pre-school period becomes a particularly important time to develop neighbourhood contacts, which may, if they are well-established endure sporadically as other areas take on a more and more time-consuming role. The revival of neighbourhood children's groups should help to encourage this. With television, the home has perhaps become more important than it used to be, however, since short periods between school, study and outside classes can more profitably be spent there than outside seeking friends.

Notes

1   Economic Welfare Bureau 1980: 23.
2   *Mama Wakatte Ne (You Understand, Don't You, Mummy)* 1981: 3.
3   Ministry of Foreign Affairs 1976: 13.
4   Maretzki & Maretzki 1963: 148.
5   *Kōseihakusho (Ministry of Welfare White Paper)* 1979: 28.
6   Aoi 1970: 24; 1976: 58; Koyano 1964: 155.
7   Koyano, *ibid.*
8   See, for example, the magazine *Mothering,* edited by Ikegami Chizuko.
9   Hara 1980: 10.
10   Norbeck & Norbeck 1956: 657.
11   Maretzki & Maretzki 1963: 150–1.
12   *Ibid.* 149–50.
13   Singer 1973: 36.
14   Maretzki & Maretzki 1963: 150.
15   Hara 1980: 10; cf. Benedict 1977: 184–5.
16   See, for example, Fukutake 1972; Hendry 1981: chapter 2; Nakane 1967; and Beardsley, Hall & Ward.
17   Hara & Wagatsuma 1974: 60.
18   Hara 1980: 9; see, for example, Johnson 1975: 52.
19   Hara & Wagatsuma 1974: 62–3; Takeuchi 1957; Sakurai 1962: 314–25; Seki 1962: 128–43; variations in such groups are discussed in Johnson 1975: 52–60.
20   *Pre-school Education in Japan* 1981: 20.

21   *Ibid.* 18; *Early Childhood Education in Japan* 1979: 99.
22   *Ibid.* 11.
23   *Ibid.* 9.
24   *Ibid.* 17; cf. *Pre-school Education in Japan* 1979: 12–13; also *Ochano-mizu Joshi Daigaku Fuzoku Yōchien Hyakunenshi* (*A Hundred Years of History of the Ochanomizu Women's University Kindergarten*).
25   *Early Childhood Education* 17, 21, 23; cf. Deasey 1978: 37, 40–1.
26   *Early Childhood Education* 19, 98.
27   *Ibid.* 73; for an incisive analysis of the Japanese system see Dore 1976: 35–50.
28   *Early Childhood Education* 31 reports 1978 average of 33.5 children per class.
29   *Early Childhood Education* 53.
30   Hara 1980: 20–1; cf. Kondo 1974.
31   Riggs 1977: 549.

1   One advantage of leaving shoes in the doorway is that it is possible to see
     who is inside before you enter. One or two children in this kindergarten
     find it difficult to summon up the courage to join such a large gathering
     (pp. 75–6)

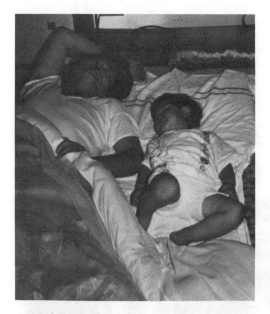

2 The 'family bed': When a new baby is born, the older child may start to sleep with father (p. 21)

3 Grandfathers taking care of small children (see e.g. p. 52)

4 The card game Takayuki, aged 3 years 10 months, and his father are playing helps to teach phonetic characters as the child has to search for a card with a particular sound written on it (see pp. 25–6)

5 When Takayuki does something naughty, his father makes him say sorry and then count up to ten

6 Mother helps Takayuki with learning to fold his own clothes (see p. 82)

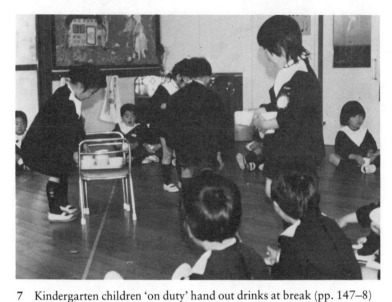

7 Kindergarten children 'on duty' hand out drinks at break (pp. 147–8)

A special snack is served at a kindergarten monthly birthday party (pp.
8 139–40)

9 The percussion band practises for sports day (pp. 142, 146)

10 Kendo lessons after school (p. 66)

9

10

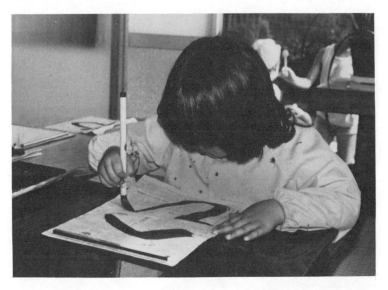

11 Calligraphy classes after school (p. 66)

Running races on sports day emphasise participation as a *representative* of the class or neighbourhood rather than for individual
12 endeavour (pp. 142–3)

13 Children often help to pull a portable shrine round the district at Shinto festivals (p. 41)

14 Children dressed up for a procession to inaugurate a new building at a Buddhist temple (p. 42)

13

14

15   Children usually play an important role in local festivals. The practice for this drumming fills the evening air for some weeks before the event itself (pp. 41–2)

Chapter Three

Aims and aspirations

To follow the discussion of the people and places involved in the rearing of small children, this chapter turns to look at the aims and objectives of the adults concerned. There will of course be individual variations in the aspirations of parents for their own children, and these will be considered shortly, but there is also a high level of agreement about some of the basic principles. Some of the broader ideas emerged in Chapter I in the discussion about the Japanese word for child-rearing, namely *shitsuke*. The more mundane content of *shitsuke* forms the subject matter of the first section of this chapter, where a fairly comprehensive picture should emerge of the objectives shared by most Japanese people involved in it. Ideals in the view of parents are of course related to these objectives, and three sections follow on 'the good child', 'shortcomings' and 'aspirations for the future', which should complement and expand the earlier section, as well as giving some idea of the range of opinion found on this subject.

The content of *shitsuke*

So important and all-embracing is this concept of *shitsuke* that it was sometimes difficult to pin people down to specific details of their practice by asking about it directly. There was a question used when interviewing mothers which mentioned the word by asking what aspects of *shitsuke* they regarded as important. Possibly it was badly phrased, although I did discuss the best way to ask about *shitsuke* with a Japanese mother, because many of the respondents found it a difficult question to answer. Some of them, particularly in Kyushu, laughed at the question and, using the verb form of the word, said that they didn't *shitsuke* their children at all, perhaps because they were too busy, or because the children learned 'naturally'. Others took the question very seriously and thought for a long time before answering. Yet others reacted by becoming rather embarrassed, as if they were not sure whether their own methods would qualify to be discussed in this context. The reason for this response may well become clearer in the next chapter, where the methods used in child rearing are discussed, because they are on the whole diffuse, rather than very organised, so that informants probably found it difficult to extract from their whole life-style particularly important aspects. However, one Japanese commentator has pointed out that *shitsuke* involves 'instinctive' (*honnōteki*) or reflective behaviour with little scope for decision or speculation.[1]

Nevertheless, from the answers which were given, a number of frequently occurring objectives did emerge, and these fall into a small number of categories, although some important aspects may cut across them. The following sections in which these are discussed are named somewhat arbitrarily and possibly could be better ordered. Especially the question of where one draws the line, if indeed there is one, between social and moral rules, is difficult, and could well be rather ethnocentrically chosen here. However, I have tried to provide enough information to allow the reader to understand the indigenous categories.

A short questionnaire issued to parents of Shirayuri Kindergarten asked again for the three things they saw as most important in their current *shitsuke* and the answers received served to confirm that there were indeed a limited number of specific objectives involved. The content of *shitsuke* as indicated by manuals of advice confirms this list, as does a handbook about day nurseries issued by Tateyama City Hall. Some of the more analytical answers obtained in the interviews revealed some underlying principles which proved to be extremely illuminating. These will be discussed towards the end of each section.

On the subject of when *shitsuke* starts, some informants reported that it is from birth, since a baby absorbs what the parents are doing even if it does not understand. Again, this will become clearer in the next chapter, when the methods are explained, because we find that the parents' own behaviour and the setting of an atmosphere are important elements. Manuals on child-rearing for mothers some-times divide their advice into sections appropriate for particular ages, where they also discuss the child's development at each stage. For example, a child's will is said to awaken during the second year so that the mother should prepare to deal with some resistance to her efforts. Ibuka advises that this is the time when the mother's duty is to guide that will carefully.[2] However, although the details vary, the categories of concern seem to persist through the stages, so the following exposition is by category, rather than by trying to move chronologically through the child's stages of development.

Greetings and other ritual phrases

Most commonly mentioned amongst the general objects of *shitsuke* at the pre-school stage were *aisatsu* or 'greetings'. In fact the term in Japanese is wider than 'greetings' so that concrete examples include words corresponding to 'sorry' and 'thank you' as well as 'good morning', 'good night' and a number of phrases fixed in conventional usage in Japan which have no equivalent at all in English. The training in this ability to communicate politely with other people does not need to wait until a child can speak, for it includes the commonly described pushing-down of the head of the baby on its mother's back into a bow of greeting, and the encouragement of a baby from an early age to respond to having its name called.

The 'reply' or *henji* is sometimes cited separately as an objective and involves eventually a clearly pronounced 'yes' (*hai*) from the child being addressed. One of the interviewees reported proudly that *hai* had been her son's first word, which he pronounced at four-to-five months, and an informant whose nine-month-old baby learned to respond in this way while we were in Japan reported the fact with jubilation to her neighbours. Later on, at kindergarten, the taking of the register is an important daily ritual when the success of the mother in this respect is used to good effect, and Vogel has seen this as the beginning of training for school when it is important that a child should be able to speak clearly in front of the whole class.[3] Before the child is old enough to go to kindergarten, adults make a game of calling its name so that it can show how well and clearly it can reply, and this was one of the skills informants sometimes had a child demonstrate to me during my research.

Daily greetings, such as 'good morning', 'good day', 'goodbye' and 'good night' are practised in a ritualised fashion in some families, and adults make a point of greeting even the smallest child so that it has an opportunity to reply and take part in interaction in public too. Apart from these there are a number of phrases used in particular situations in Japan. When leaving and entering one's own house, there are fixed expressions of farewell and arrival, sometimes used with children even if there is no one in the house actually to greet, so that this becomes part of a ritual of entry and exit. In other people's houses there are different phrases to be used, as there are phrases for the occupants of the house to welcome and see off visitors. These are invariable and quite ritualised and since the 'home' ones are reserved for members of the family, they serve to distinguish them clearly from outsiders.

'Thank you' and 'sorry' are slightly different in that they are less automatic and ritualistic, but they are often mentioned together as important things to form part of early training. Some informants report that 'thank you' is not used much within the immediate family where certain activities are expected routinely amongst the members, but instead the word is used to express obligation to outsiders, including perhaps grandparents, so that this emphasises again the distinction between members of the immediate family and other people with whom the child comes into contact. 'Sorry' is one of the few words that mothers make considerable fuss about having the child pronounce clearly in a situation in which it is judged to have offended, because harmony amongst children is an important ideal from very early, and this word and its acceptance makes it possible for a situation of harmony to be restored.

These 'greetings' in fact serve to demonstrate and emphasise a number of basic categories and values of the society at large. The child is made aware of its own identity in its unique ability to reply to its personal name, but it is reminded of the relationship it has with other people to whom certain phrases are appropriately used in certain situations. Members of the house are distinguished quite clearly from members of the outside world, but it is clear that other people have houses where respect is due to the space inside, and special behaviour is called for. With regard to personal relations, there is an emphasis on harmony and it is important to express obligation in certain situations.

Etiquette

The inculcation of 'manners' or 'etiquette' (*reigi sahō*) into a child, also mentioned frequently as an objective of *shitsuke,* includes all the above 'greetings' and more, since the term has a meaning almost as wide as that of *shitsuke* itself. Some aspects of it are, like *shitsuke,* concerned with the positioning of the body, and as well as learning to bow, a child is encouraged to sit properly in formal situations. Thus, when visiting, or receiving guests, the proper posture is a kneeling position with the buttocks resting evenly on the heels. If one is entreated to relax, boys may sit cross-legged and girls give relief to their bent legs by sitting to one side or the other. In fact, small children are rarely expected to maintain a formal position for any length of time, but this is an appropriate stage for a child to show, if only briefly, that it knows the proper way to behave. In kindergarten, too, there is an expected way for children to sit, for example with their hands clasped over their knees, and the often quite hard floor is used on certain occasions even in establishments which provide tables and chairs for normal use. Stylised movements of the body are also often practised daily, usually to the accompaniment of music from the piano or records. Thus, it can be seen that the literal control of the body is indeed an early concern.

The height of bad manners in Japan, unthinkable for Japanese, would be to enter a house with one's shoes on. Although shoe training is not mentioned specifically by many people discussing *shitsuke,* probably because it is just too basic, this is one of the first things which must really be insisted upon. Its importance is witnessed by the use of a pair of shoes as an illustration on the front cover of a collection of essays on the topic of *shitsuke.*[4] The removal of shoes on entering a house, and the donning of them on leaving, is concerned partly with cleanliness, which falls into the subject matter of a following section, but it also becomes a ritual which creates a clear distinction between the inside and the outside of the home. As toddlers learn the basic principle of the shoe habit, they are also encouraged to turn round and tidy their shoes before they carry on into the house. To do this properly, the shoes should also be turned round so that they may be stepped into neatly as one leaves, and so that the row of shoes at the entrance to a house is neat and orderly. In winter, at least, one then dons a pair of slippers. To do all this daintily is quite an art, as foreigners find when they practice rather clumsily in the early stages. In practice, little girls often become much more adept at it than boys, the former stopping to tidy a whole row of shoes, while the latter rush in to get on with some other activity.

Another distinction which seems to be inculcated in the early training of good manners is one between the upper and lower part of the body. The lower extreme is covered in objects which are too dirty to bring into the house, and the whole of the lower part is tucked away when one sits formally. The upper part is that used to bow and show respect, and the word for 'above' (*ue*) is applied to people who are considered superior, literally 'above one's eyes' (*meue*). There is another little aspect of good manners in Japan which seems to confirm the importance of this distinction, and that is the unseemliness attached to the revealing of one's umbilicus, a convenient point to be regarded as the boundary between upper and lower body. Some people warn that a belly button revealed will be struck by lightning, or removed by the deity of thunder and lightning. There are even little garments for toddlers, to be worn in the height of summer, which cover very little else, and consequently involve rather a complicated arrangment of ties at the back. They are not seen a great deal, it is true, but perhaps that is because the T-shirts which have become popular do much the same job. Belly buttons are certainly not shown off freely, and I suspect that it may have something to do with the symbolic importance of the distinction between upper and lower in Japanese society.

Food and meals

The head of Shirayuri said that she could tell how good the *shitsuke* of her children was when she saw them eating. This is a time when the English too claim to be able to assess manners, but there are certain differences. A Japanese mother who had lived in England told me that she thought the Japanese are perhaps stricter with their children in this respect than the English are. The head of the kindergarten went on to say that well-brought up children sit properly at meals, don't play around or even talk, and they eat up all their food. This is a summary of what is expected, but a consideration of all the comments about eating reveals some quite elaborate ritual as well.

First of all, the meal, or even just a snack, is separated from other activities by the use of a small ritual before and after it. Children are usually encouraged to wash their hands before and after eating, which also has to do with hygiene, but before they begin to eat they should say another stereotypical phrase of thanks (*itadakimasu*), and, before they leave the table at the end, they should say another phrase of appreciation (*gochisōsama deshita*). The grace said at some Christian tables may serve a similar ritual function, but the Japanese phrases are much more universally used than grace is said in Christian houses. In kindergarten, too, children sit with their break or lunch in front of them until everyone is ready to begin eating, when they chorus the appropriate phrase. During the meal, itself, while silence is not enforced, children are encouraged to eat as quickly as possible, avoid spilling anything on the floor, and finish up everything laid in front of them. In the kindergarten, where sometimes they actually eat off the floor, each child brings a napkin which is laid out carefully to mark its own space, the lunch box and drink being placed in a fixed way on top of it. There is also a proper way to hold the bowl and chopsticks, but these are arts learnt gradually as the child becomes more competent.

The whole business is taught in stages, as the child reaches the age thought appropriate, and one of the manuals lists aims for each of the first four years. At one year, the child should learn to feed itself, at first using a spoon. By three, it should be transferring to chopsticks, when it should also be saying the phrase at the end of the meal and avoiding spilling things on the floor. By four, it should be saying the phrases both at the beginning and the end, and should also be competent with chopsticks.[5] It is interesting that matters of manual dexterity are considered on a par with ritual phrases. It was noticeable that quite tiny children spill very little food on the floor, and since mothers tend to avoid coercion at meal times, I think it must be associated with the respect accorded food, emphasised by this ritual separation of eating from other activities. The low table, where food is eaten, is an area children are discouraged from climbing on to, the phrase 'that's where food is eaten' being used as an amiable rationale for it. The use of napkins to mark out a space for food may be seen in the same light. There seems also to be some folklore attached to the wasting of even 'one grain of rice' (*hitotsubu*), which is said to make one go blind, literally 'one's eyes would be smashed' (*tsubureru*), a play on the similar pronunciation, though the words are not related. Nowadays there is also a lot of literature available for mothers on the making up of a balanced diet, important for maintaining healthy bodies, always emphasised as the number one concern of *shitsuke,* which is another aspect of the beautification of the body.

As children reach the age when they should be capable of the basic niceties of eating, their parents still sometimes mention food habits as an aspect of *shitsuke,* now a matter of sitting properly, the discouragement of likes and dislikes in food, the finishing up of what is available, and the discouragement of other activities while eating. Some families insist that the television be turned off during meals, but there may be a Western influence at work here, since they sometimes seemed to think that this was a practice I might approve of. It is in keeping with the separation of eating from other activities, but many Japanese eat in front of the television as a regular habit, and it seems to be custom to have a television in the room where meals are taken.

It should perhaps be emphasised at this stage that while the ritual associated with eating is observed widely in Japan, there are of course variations in daily practice from one family to another. Especially in the country, where parents are trying to work with children around, snacks such as crackers, crisps and sweets are used to keep children occupied, and the same principle is applied on trains and in other public places to keep children out of trouble. It is probably significant that the head of Shirayuri Kindergarten, who was concerned with the high-class nature of her establishment, chose eating as a way to assess the *shitsuke* of her children. As in England, there is no doubt a relationship between social class and manners expected at meals, and it was often the better-off families who mentioned eating as an aspect of *shitsuke* with which they were especially concerned.

Cleanliness and order

Attitudes to dirt and cleanliness are often so early instilled into us that we tend to think of them as rather natural and universal, until we happen to travel abroad and discover that views elsewhere are quite different. A common reaction is to class foreigners as dirty, although in the case of Japan outside observers usually comment on the cleanliness, which was seen in a period of wartime antagonism as an example of 'pathological compulsiveness'.[6] Even academics find it hard to escape their own expectations in this respect, it seems. Mary Douglas has shown most convincingly that ideas about dirt and pollution are concerned with order and classification,[7] and the Japanese case is no exception to her general principles. The discussion above about the custom of removing shoes gives some idea of the possibilities involved.[8] It is rationalised as being concerned with hygiene and cleanliness of the house, but it seemed important enough to be classed here in the section on manners. Other ideas about cleanliness and order are less revered, perhaps, but they also point to important aspects of the system of classification in Japanese society.

One of the words used by informants to refer to habits of cleanliness in connection with *shitsuke* was *seiketsu,* which may be translated as 'neatness' and 'purity' as well as 'cleanliness', which gives a measure of the value of the concept, as well as adding justification to the consideration of cleanliness together with order. Another word used was *seiri seiton,* which is more exclusively concerned with the maintenance of order. More specifically, parents would often say that they taught their children to put away their toys, and *katazuke,* the word used to announce this activity, is often accorded the honorific prefix *o,* which lends it something of a ritual air. The nature of Japanese houses, where the same space may be used for different activities such as sleeping, eating, playing and watching television, makes it necessary to tidy things away after each event, whereas in Western houses one may move to another room and leave tidying for later.

Other specific customs mentioned were sometimes described as concerned with hygiene (*eiseishūkan*), but details were interesting. The washing of hands before and after meals has been mentioned already, but the other time mentioned when hands should be washed

79

is when one comes into the house, and this may be accompanied by a washing out of the mouth or gargling. This emphasises the distinction already discussed in connection with shoes between the clean inside of the house and the dirt or pollution of the outside world. Children returning from kindergarten or day nursery are usually expected to change their clothes at this time too, and there is a word to refer to smart clean clothes donned for a special outing which has the literal meaning of 'going out' (*odekake*). The bath was not cited as having anything in particular to do with *shitsuke,* but there is a definite way of behaving in a Japanese bath and children are aware of the rules very early. They also enjoy the ritual element attached to it and wallow in the 'good feeling' expected after a bath, when a tasty cool drink may well be forthcoming. The usual time for a bath is before retiring, which separates daytime and night-time, but on special occasions such as festivals and other evening outings a bath is usually taken first, and in the hot summer, cool Japanese garments are often worn outside.

Teeth-cleaning is sometimes mentioned as a habit to be taught to children and this comes surprisingly late from a Western point of view, a manual for mothers putting the accomplishment as appropriate for a five-year-old to learn, whereas gargling is recommended to be mastered at three.[9] The number of small children with bad teeth would appear to attest to a lack of concern in this matter, although some Japanese apparently claim that the problem is a genetic one.

Some kindergartens insist that children keep a toothbrush on the premises and clean their teeth at certain times, thereby compensating, they say, for lax attitudes at home. Public programmes of dental care, including visits from dentists to schools and kindergartens, and talks to members of the PTA, may alter this attitude, however.

In general there is a high degree of awareness of the association between cleanliness and health, indeed, there is a saying which threatens 'dirty' people with 'dirty diseases'.[10] There is certainly a great emphasis on the importance of being healthy. Children who are able to attend every single day of the term at Shirayuri Kindergarten are given a special 'reward' at the breaking-up ceremony, which cannot help but attach a certain amount of shame to being off sick. Hara and Wagatsuma relate what they describe as a 'prejudice' (*henken*) against people with injuries and ill-health to the fact that they are unable to fulfil their role as a complete 'one helping of a person'.[11]

The earliest part of *shitsuke* indicated specifically by some informants is toilet training, which again is a matter of both cleanliness and order. The aspect of cleanliness is self-evident, but the approach in Japan, which was described in Chapter I, is also concerned with the creation of regular habits, which, as will be seen in the next chapter, is a general principle used in *shitsuke*. When I took my younger son for his eighteen-month check-up with the municipal authorities in Tateyama, I discussed my problems in toilet training with the public health nurse there. She advised me to persist in having the same person take him at the same time each day to the same place, which would surely bring eventual success. The place chosen for toilet training in Japan is also an interesting indication of classification again, for the toilet itself is a rather dangerous gaping hole in some houses. Although potties have become quite popular recently, the custom which predated them was to hold the child out over the edge of the verandah, which provides another association of the outside of the house with uncleanliness. It is also customary in Japanese houses for a special pair of slippers to be kept in the toilet, so that dirt from the floor is not carried to the other rooms, and this again symbolically puts this 'dirty' place outside the main part of the home, where it still physically is in some country areas.

Another part of early training mentioned by some informants with young babies is the need to teach them what they may and may not put in their mouths. This is partly a matter of distinguishing clean and dirty objects, but also concerned with the danger of swallowing small things. The danger of the hot stove is another thing a baby learns to be aware of, and the word for danger is often used to dissuade a baby from some action. One mother pointed out that it was convenient that her rubbish bucket lid hurt if the baby caught its hand in it, for it was more difficult to put the child off a place by just saying it was dirty. The association of dirt with danger is recognised in terms of hygiene, but anthropologists like Mary Douglas argue that it goes much deeper than the recent understanding of bacteria.[12] In all these early concerns, the baby is gradually becoming aware of its own identity and separateness, emphasised by activities associating the boundaries of the body with ideas of dirt and danger.

Doing things for oneself

As a child grows up a little, it is encouraged to distinguish its own belongings from those of others and to take care of them itself. A common element of *shitsuke* mentioned by mothers of three-to-five year-olds is this encouragement of a child to do things for itself. This begins with learning to eat its own food, although a mother may continue helping a child to clean the plate and eat tidily. It is also gradually encouraged to go to the toilet by itself. As it begins to be able to change its own clothes, the caretaker aims to teach it to fold up and put away things it will need for the next day. Similarly, the child should know where its toys go and put them away when it finishes playing with them. As the child gets older, one of the things mentioned is to teach it how to take care of things and look after them, generally to take responsibility for its own belongings. Some add that it is important for a child to finish a job, which includes clearing everything away. This is all concerned with order, but the wording of the phrase used by parents (*jibun no koto wa jibun de suru*), also emphasises the fact that a child is doing its own things for itself, thus adding an element of awareness of identity again. This aspect of *shitsuke* is often cited by young mothers as something which the older generation in a family is uncooperative about, and kindergarten teachers comment that children from extended households are often less able to do things for themselves because their grandparents do so much for them.

Morality

The encouragement of independence is certainly not to be confused with selfishness, however, and another common aim of *shitsuke* mentioned by informants is to teach the child to think of others, be kind and sympathetic to them, and to avoid causing people trouble or annoyance. This starts early when a tiny child is discouraged from taking things from other children, throwing things at them, and pushing, scratching and biting. Slightly older children are taught to be kind to the smaller ones, who 'are not yet able to understand', and to lend them their toys. If they are remiss in this they are exhorted to think how they would like to receive the behaviour they are meting out. From about three years, when rationale is deemed to penetrate, it is explained to children that they are not alone in the world and they should not do to others what they would not like to have done to themselves. More specifically, they should not annoy or tease other children, with whom they should try at all times to play harmoniously, whoever they may be.

Sometimes it is a specific aim of parents that their children should become skilled at understanding the feelings of others, and one parent hoped to teach her small child to read people's faces. Examples of wider aims of this sort were 'to cultivate sentiments', 'to have pity', and 'to have the ability to be moved or inspired'. For children of about five or six years, parents sometimes talked about respect for elders, in particular teachers, parents and old people, and others said they taught their children to be kind to old people. Certainly it was commonly emphasised that one should not put upon people or take advantage of the kindness of strangers. Co-operation was also mentioned by one informant, but this becomes more important when children enter a formal group at nursery or kindergarden.

The child's individual personality is not to be neglected, however, and some aims of *shitsuke* emphasise this by encouraging the child to express his or her own will clearly, or to analyse and express their own feelings about something. Some informants mentioned specific ideals such as 'autonomy' and 'self-reliance' as qualities they wanted to encourage in their children, but there is also an emphasis on 'self-control'. Perhaps a rather modern aim, mentioned by one or two people, is the development of 'spontaneity' in their children. All these words begin with the same character for 'self', and again, indicate a concern with the awareness of identity, not to be lost in the emphasis on thinking of others, but nevertheless adding to the understanding of the identity and needs of other people in the world. They also emphasise an aim stated clearly by two informants that children should think for themselves and be able thereby to behave in the proper way.

Further personal characteristics thought to be important to develop are loosely translated into English as 'endurance' and 'honesty'. The first is *gaman* in Japanese, which may also be glossed as 'patience' and 'tolerance', and one informant listed not being fussy about food, looking after things, keeping promises and 'tenacity' (*ganbaruko ni naru*) as examples of *shitsuke* concerned with *gaman*. More commonly people mentioned things like having the patience and endurance to finish things, the persistence to keep trying in the face of apparent failure, and the general ability to try as hard as possible in whatever one does (*nandemo isshō-kenmei*). The development of the ability to concentrate on things was also mentioned specifically by one or two people.

With regard to 'honesty' this is rather an English interpretation, because the Japanese words used were closer to 'not to tell lies' and 'to keep promises', which covers only part of the English concept. Keeping promises (*yakusoku*) is important, because promises are used quite often by parents in the child-rearing process as a means to explain required behaviour and enter into a type of small contract with the child. It is one stage further than expecting a child to 'listen' to what is being said to it. A lie or fabrication is equivalent to the breaking of a promise and a feeling for the seriousness of this misdemeanor is indicated by a little rhyme most children know, which runs:

Yakusoku genman	If your promise
Uso tsuitara	Turns out to be a lie
Hari senbon	You'll have to swallow
Nomasu.	A thousand needles.

Discrimination

Finally, at a more abstract level, the teaching of 'discrimination' or 'distinction' (*kejime*) is sometimes mentioned as an object of *shitsuke* and this concept would seem to incorporate a number of the more specific things discussed already. In particular the ability to distinguish between good and bad is mentioned, but there are also the distinctions I have pointed out between various activities, such as eating and playing, and the wider ones between the inside and the outside of the house. The words *uchi* and *soto* are applied in the last case and may also be applied to members, objects and ways of the house in the former case, and distinguished from people, objects and customs of the outside world by the prefix *yoso no*. Informants mentioned the importance of distinguishing between work and play, or study and play as a child grows up a little, and I think this teaching is aided by the use of small rituals of cleanliness and greeting.

A particularly important distinction also mentioned specifically is that between self and others, or between the things one wants to do oneself and the limits imposed on these by the things other people want to do. Indeed, one informant elaborated the discussion of *kejime* by saying that it was concerned with boundaries (*genkai*) and limits (*gendo*), and the ability to impose these in an appropriate way. She said that the ultimate aim in personal relations is to achieve *kyōchō,* which combines the English concepts of 'co-operation', 'harmony' and 'conciliation', and it is for the sake of this aim that *kejime* is necessary. One must understand oneself and work out for oneself the behaviour appropriate to achieve *kyōchō* in a particular situation. Thus one must also learn to discriminate between different types of people, that is those to whom respect is appropriate, those to whom one should be especially thoughtful and kind, and those with whom one may play and cooperate in a more or less equal manner. Indeed, *shitsuke* is concerned with learning the important categories of society and the way in which the Japanese world is classified. This subject is discussed more comprehensively in Chapter VI.

Qualities of character

Having considered some of the specific objectives of *shitsuke,* we turn now to examine some of the general qualities which are admired in the first place, and discouraged in the second, in small children. These sections are based largely on the answers to a question about 'temperament' on the forms filled out by parents entering their children into two kindergartens, and the answers to questions in the interviews about what children are praised for and what made their mothers angry respectively. On the kindergarten forms, parents were asked to fill in a section on their child's nature or 'temperament' (*seishitsu*), which was divided into a space for 'good points' and one for 'bad points' or 'points to be corrected'. Under 'good points' were a number of frequently recurring terms in both the public Tateyama Kindergarten and the private Shirayuri Kindergarten. These will be considered in the first part of this section, whereas the shortcomings will form the subject matter of the second part. Some of the answers to the question on what children are praised for reflect the expected 'good points', but on the whole, they tended to refer more to specific activities and thus relate rather to the previous section. For this reason they will be considered first.

The good child

Some parents actually began the answer to this question by saying that they did not often praise their children as they thought too much praise a bad thing, but many of them then went on to provide one or two exceptions to this statement. In fact, out of forty-eight answers, with seventy-seven reasons for praise, there were really only about ten different things which were mentioned. In the case of tiny babies, praise was offered for little accomplishments such as clapping of hands, singing, dancing and so forth, and as children were being toilet trained they were praised as they reached the stage of asking to go to the toilet. The former activity could probably be classed in the more general category of trying hard and doing something well (*gambatte nanika seikō dekiru*), and the latter in the ability to do something oneself. As the child grows up a little, the accomplishments tend to be concerned with kindergarten, and later, school, although in the interim period the ability to dress oneself was mentioned. Very much related to the previous section is praise for saying greetings nicely, for eating properly, for putting things away, and, most commonly mentioned, for being kind or generous to friends or younger siblings. More even than all of these, however, children were praised when they helped their mothers, or ran little errands, especially if they did such things without being asked. If they responded quickly when asked to do something, this was also sometimes deemed worthy of praise. Finally, one informant said she praised her child for keeping promises. It can be seen, then, that praise may reinforce the *shitsuke* discussed in the previous section, but since an overwhelming majority mentioned help, this does rather imply that children have to do a little more than normally expected before praise is forthcoming.

The qualities mentioned in the kindergarten forms as 'good points' fall into a rather different level of behaviour since they are concerned with 'nature' and 'temperament'. This time the most commonly mentioned quality was health and vitality. The three or four words which recur again and again in these forms have a range of meaning from health through cheerfulness, brightness, happiness, sunny disposition, liveliness to vivacity and vigour. The emphasis on health was mentioned in the previous section, but a child should also be bright and cheerful, even cheeky, and efforts are made not to dampen this quality in tiny children.

The next most frequently mentioned word is rather difficult to translate into English, but corresponds in a Japanese view to where we in the West would probably expect 'obedience'. Indeed, 'obedience' is one of the dictionary translations offered for *sunao*, but I think it is important to discuss the different range of meaning as this is one of the most basic differences in expectations of Japanese and Western children. Other dictionary translations of *sunao* are gentle, meek, submissive, tame, tractable, compliant, yielding, honest and frank. Doi adds guileless, straightforward and amenable.[13] The characters used to write *sunao* are composed of an emphatic prefix and a character meaning 'honesty', 'frankness' and 'straightness', also used in the verb *naosu*, which has meanings of to mend, to reform, to correct, to cure and to straighten.

Hara and Wagatsuma have discussed the difficulties of translating *sunao* into English and suggest 'upright' and 'compliant' as close in meaning, but note that there is more involved, and that this is related to the concept of *amae*, the 'dependence' or 'passive love' mentioned in Chapter I. They suggest that if a child receives enough love from a parent than it will be *sunao*, since reliance and trust will be established so that the child will comply with the parents' directives and advice. If the parent is successful in this respect, the child will also listen to and comply with the instructions of other older people to whom respect should be accorded.[14] When a child refuses to do things it can or should be able to do at a certain age, it is said to be *amaeteru* or an *amaekko*, which suggests an excess of dependence.

This is often translated into English as 'spoilt', but evidently has quite different connotations since the English term is usually applied to a child who has received an excess of attention, whereas in a Japanese view giving a small child a lot of attention in the early stages is thought to encourage trust and thereby 'compliance'. Compliance is closer to what is sought in a Japanese child than the unqualified obedience we might expect in the West. As the psychologist Lanham observed, 'mere obedience as such carries no virtue. Obedience that occurs spontaneously, or at least willingly, is sought'. The compliance too must be willing, it seems, for she goes on, 'Mere compliance is deemed of little or no value'.[15]

Sometimes together with *sunao,* but also often separately, two other words recur frequently and these were those mentioned as part of *shitsuke,* discussed above under the section on 'morality'. They are *yasashii,* which is translated into English as gentle, kind, tender, graceful and affectionate, and *omoiyari,* which is a kind of sympathy or fellow-feeling. Both qualities are conducive to thinking of others and avoiding the causing of trouble or discord in relations with other people. Thus they are regarded as good in the sense of aiding and incorporating the ideals of moral development.

Other phrases which recurred in the forms did so with much less frequency than those already discussed, which seems to imply a high level of agreement on good qualities expected in children. Some of the others reinforce the objectives of *shitsuke.* A common one was the ability to play with or get on with anyone, and related to this, not being bashful or shy of strangers. Another was 'to know their own mind', but a child with this quality was often criticised for it under 'bad points' as 'having a strong will'.

One aspect of good character which was mentioned more frequently on the public kindergarten forms than on the private ones was 'helpful to parents'. Phrases which occurred only on the private kindergarten forms were 'good at understanding' and 'remembers things quickly' which suggests a more academic orientation and less practical aspect of the aspirations of the better-off parents. Some answers in both groups mentioned the ability to do things for oneself, to concentrate, or be enthusiastic about something, and to persist and persevere to the end of a project. Others put down specific aspects of *shitsuke* such as cleaning teeth regularly, putting things away, replying well to having their name called, and being quick to apologise. Other aspects of character which were mentioned more than once, but only by a few, were curiosity, neatness, carefulness, constructiveness, methodicalness, a liking for animals and books, and an ability to play alone.

Shortcomings

The common view that a child is born without sin should perhaps be reiterated here. The head of Shirayuri Kindergarten was fond of reminding teachers and parents alike that a small child is 'completely white'. Mischief she interpreted as mere curiosity to see what would happen, and if there were problems it was the fault of parents, teachers and other surrounding influences, since the child itself could never be bad. Not surprisingly, the form filled in on entry to this kindergarten did not have a space for 'bad points', but for 'points to be corrected', or more accurately perhaps, 'to be straightened out', since the verb used was *naosu* which has the same root as *sunao*. The Tateyama Kindergarten form did have a space for 'bad points', however, and it also had one for 'points particularly in need of correction/straightening'. This section is based on the responses to these sections on the forms, and on answers to the interview question about what made mothers angry.

The interview answers to this question were usually rather short, although most caretakers did admit to getting cross from time to time. Those who said they never got angry were either mothers of small babies, who were said not to be old enough for that yet, or those who had outside jobs and didn't see their children during the day. However, I only rarely saw a Japanese mother show her anger – some said they wouldn't anyway outside the privacy of their own homes – and there was again quite a small number of apparent causes. The most common, especially in the country sample, was when children don't listen to what they've been told. Perhaps linked to this were breaking promises and telling lies. Mothers were also angry if the child did something dangerous. Other causes of anger were direct contraventions of *shitsuke* such as being fussy about food or not eating it properly, thinking only of their own things, quarrelling, causing trouble to people and annoying a small sibling or animal. One or two parents mentioned the lack of help as being a reason for anger, and in the country a few mentioned the taking of food or money without asking.

By a long way the most frequent answer on the kindergarten forms was that a child was selfish or thought only of its own concerns. This shortcoming is expected of small children, but should be rectified by adults in moral training about the importance of thinking of others. Thus it is partly the fault of the adult if the training had not yet been entirely effective. The word most often used for this shortcoming is *wagamama,* the second half of which (*mama)* means 'as it is', which implies that the first half (*waga*), which means 'own' or 'self', is left unsocialised to consider others. Thus, it is not really a bad aspect of character, just an untrained one.

Also often mentioned was a word which may be translated as 'cry baby', again an interesting combination of characters, possibly to be interpreted as laying the blame outside the child itself. The word is *nakimushi,* where *naki* means 'to cry' and *mushi* is the 'insect' discussed in Chapter I, which may get into a child and affect its behaviour. However, informants suggested that it could also imply that the child is behaving like an insect by crying so much.[16] Again this is a point which should be rectified if possible. Although babies are picked up and soothed when they cry, by the time they enter kindergarten, crying children are rather ignored or dubbed 'strange' (*okashii*). However, it is significant that it was such a frequent response, because a child who cries is difficult to deal with since it is said to be a sin to make a child cry.

Other qualities of character which were often mentioned in the section of the form were also ones which caretakers found difficult to deal with. They included shortness of temper, impatience, obstinacy, stubbornness and strong will. Some also cited an inability to express an opinion clearly, however. Very common was the word which is translated into English as 'spoilt', but which has a rather different meaning as was discussed in the previous section, namely *amaekko,* a child who refuses to do things it can or should be able to do at a certain age. Thus it can be seen that the shortcomings, taken together, represent the opposite qualities of those most commonly cited in the previous section as good points, namely cheerfulness, compliancy and thought for others.

Again, specific contraventions of *shitsuke* such as not eating properly, not speaking properly, and not persevering with things, were mentioned occasionally, as were an inability to play with other children and an unwillingness to lend toys. Shyness, cowardice, and a retiring nature were also mentioned quite often as shortcomings, but a rough, wild temperament was also criticised. In the Tateyama Kindergarten's section for 'points particularly in need of rectifying', some very specific habits regarded as bad were entered such as thumb-sucking, waiting too long before urinating, biting and left-handedness. One answer in this section was indicative of an otherwise uncommon distinction at this stage between the expectations of boys and girls. It said simply, 'he's a boy so there are no points I want to correct'. In the next section the male-female distinction is much more clear.

Aspirations for the future

One of the questions included in the interviews was 'what kind of person do you want your child to become?' Hara and Wagatsuma have suggested that this is one area which has changed little since pre-industrial times.[17] They cite the ideals of compliancy and harmonious behaviour which have already been discussed, but they also mention another aspiration which is commonly mentioned in the folklore as an aim of *shitsuke,* namely to bring people up to be ordinary or average, just like other people (*jūninnami*). A saying which summaries this idea is 'a sticking out nail should be knocked in and a bent one straightened', and it used to be the duty of the whole community to discourage people who appeared to be trying to be different.[18] Several informants did mention phrases which represent this attitude in answer to my question so the aim does not seem to have disappeared. It is rather hard for a Western observer to reconcile this view with the educational ambitions they hear that mothers have nowadays for their children, but one informant explained that the two aims are not incompatible since individuals can be very successful in their own spheres, but still remain ordinary in their everyday relations with neighbours and relatives. Perhaps 'ordinary' is the best word to use in English to translate the various Japanese words used in this context, because the other dictionary definitions, 'mediocre' and 'average' have rather derogatory connotations not associated with the Japanese ones.

However, there were also respondents who denied they wanted their children to be even 'ordinary', saying that they hoped rather to encourage an individualistic character. One mother explained that while many Japanese say in public that they want only for their child to be average, in private they would admit higher ideals. She herself elaborated no mean ambitions for her children. Another mother described how her husband would console himself when his daughter was difficult with the phrase, 'well, it's good enough if she's average', as if it were a kind of fall-back consolation if children don't achieve their parents' ambitions. A high-school student listening to one of my interviews said she thought all mothers say when their children are small that they will be happy if their child is healthy, but as they grow up, these same mothers develop higher ideals.

In fact, this was a question which elicited a wide range of responses from parents, illustrating clear differences in aspirations for boys and girls, and quite wide variations according to socio-economic circumstances. Commonly recurring in all areas were the qualities of character discussed in previous sections such as thoughtfulness, kindness, the ability to get on with anyone, and the avoidance of being a burden to other people.[19] For girls, in particular, parents frequently mentioned the word *yasashii,* which has translations such as 'gentle', 'meek' and 'tender', as well as 'kind' and 'affectionate', and other qualities sought were charm, sensible judgement, integrity, and understanding of the pain or suffering of others. Some parents said specifically that they hoped their daughters would marry at the appropriate age and be good wives. However, several mothers, as opposed to fathers, also said that they hoped their daughters would have a career of their own so that they could if necessary be independent. In one family, the father said he hoped that his son would be strong-minded, but that this was not important for his daughter, whereupon his wife disagreed and said that their daughter too might well need this quality.

In general, the list of aspirations for boys was somewhat longer and more varied than that for girls, including qualities of courage, steadfastness, resoluteness, responsibility and manliness. Specific careers were sometimes mentioned, the most common being medicine, which is very lucrative and prestigious in Japan, but other parents said that they hoped only that their son would know his own mind and do what he personally wanted to do. While some parents aspired for their sons to be rich, celebrated and successful, others said they would prefer them not to be too different from themselves.

Members of continuing families were often concerned that at least one of their sons should be able to follow in their footsteps, particularly where there was a family business or other occupation. Thus families of doctors, who had invested considerable income in the construction of a private hospital, hoped that their son or sons would be able to make the grade and continue the line, just as much as did farmers whose forbears had tilled the same plots of land for generations. One farming grandfather pointed to a house across the road, where an only son had gained admission to a prestigious university and gone on to get a job with one of the best companies in the country, and shook his head sadly about the fate of the thriving farm land and its ageing workers. However, others claim, at least in public, that they don't want to inhibit their children in this way, that they will be happy if they do what they want and perhaps fulfil a useful purpose in society.

Parents of nuclear families with no responsibilities to an older generation and no occupation to be continued were able to be quite philosophical and fanciful. They wanted both their sons and daughters to be, for example, self-reliant, independent and harmonious, to be intelligent, but not forced beyond their capabilities, to have a wide range of feeling, not to be prejudiced, to be successful, but without stepping on other people's toes. One couple wanted their children to develop just one thing they could do better than anyone else, but another was concerned that their children should not be different from other children. One mother hoped that her son would be rich – perhaps a pilot – another that her children would remember to be good to their parents, another that they would enjoy life, be able to look inside themselves and understand.

Aspirations which were mentioned particularly in the country sample were often simpler – to be healthy, first of all, then to be good, serious, upright people who were cheerful, likeable, and had the ability to talk to and get on with anyone. Some said specifically that they did not need luxury or learning though there was still concern that children should know and understand what they want to do. There was mention here too of being ordinary as a sufficient aim, but this was by no means limited to the country sample and many urban families, nuclear and extended, volunteered such information as well. Those few whose aims were specifically for individuality tended to be people with a high level of education,[20] or those who had had some experience abroad. One or two such people also hoped that their children would develop an international interest or a desire to travel, one being a mother who had studied English to degree level but who had married before she had a chance to travel herself.

It is rather a small sample from which to make valid generalisations, and it does illustrate quite a range of views, but one or two concluding remarks might be made. It seems that some rather traditional values are still being upheld quite widely, at least in public statements about aspirations for children. These might have been even stronger had the comments been made in a different context, since at times a Western interviewer tends to elicit remarks which the interviewee thinks appropriate. Many of the answers reinforce ideals extracted from other sources and discussed in previous sections of this chapter. A Western influence would appear to be evident, particularly in the emphasis on individual achievement and the encouragement of some independence and spontaneity of thought and action.

However, I think that this research was carried out at a time of some reaction to Westernisation and the answers perhaps reflect this mood. Many mothers were concerned with a lack of discipline amongst children – the press was full of violence in schools – and grandparents talked nostalgically about the greater discipline in their youth. Some mothers, particularly in cities, were looking towards Europe, where they had heard that discipline is stronger, but others are beginning to realise the value of some of their own traditional ways. There had been much publicity also about the detrimental effect of the competitive aspects of the education system, and parents are perhaps wary of being too overtly ambitious for their children, since undue success is anyway likely to undermine harmony with their neighbours. It is not without significance that individual ambition is maintained at a lower level, at least in these early stages of a child's development.

Notes

1   Inoguchi 1962: 220.
2   Ibuka 1976.
3   Vogel 1979: 168.
4   Matsubara and Satō 1976.
5   *Yōji no Kokoroe* (*Understanding Early Childhood*): 9.
6   La Barre 1962: 342.
7   See, for example, Douglas 1970.
8   I have discussed this in more detail in Hendry 1984, and Ohnuki-Tierney relates the topic to Japanese notions of germs (1984: chapter 2).
9   *Yōji no Kokoroe*: 11.
10   Hara & Wagatsuma 1974: 66; see also Ohnuki-Tierney *op. cit.*
11   *Ibid.*
12   Douglas *op. cit.* 1970.
13   Doi 1973B: 59.
14   Hara & Wagatsuma 1974: 153–5; cf. De Vos 1973: 47–8.
15   Lanham 1966: 324.
16   A similar etymology is found in the word *yowamushi,* coward or weakling, but I have not discussed attitudes to this word with informants.
17   Hara & Wagatsuma 1974: 143.
18   *Ibid.* p. 57; cf. Sato 1976: 25; Inoguchi 1962: 220.
19   These aspirations are very similar to those sought by the teachers interviewed by Shigaki (1983: 16).
20   Cf. Smith and Schooler 1978, who find in their research in Kobe a correlation between level of education and individualistic values, which they relate more generally to environmental complexity.

Chapter Four

Techniques of training: home and neighbourhood

This chapter addresses itself to the means used to try and accomplish the aims and objectives set out in Chapter III. It is concerned largely with the first two arenas of socialisation, namely the home and neighbourhood, although some of the general principles may be applied more widely. This will be illustrated in the following chapter where the kindergarten and day nursery will be considered in detail. Many writers discussing child-rearing have commented on techniques used in the Japanese case and this chapter will also bring together their comments where they seem to be valid, as well as making use of relevant interview material and less systematic observations of the behaviour of caretakers. The advice provided in manuals, and by experts on child-training is also drawn on here.

General aspects of the methods used by adults looking after small children will be considered in the first part of the chapter, when it will be seen that the whole lifestyle of caretakers becomes involved. This will be followed by a consideration of the sanctions used to induce conformity to the norms expected by society. Here I draw on some of Radcliffe Brown's system of classification of sanctions. For example, positive sanctions are concerned with the rewarding of good behaviour, and negative ones with the punishment of behaviour regarded as bad or anti-social. These sanctions may be more or less organised, the most organised ones being formulated into specific rewards or punishments, the least organised ones being general expressions of approval or disapproval.[1] The latter are termed diffuse sanctions, and, in the case of Japanese child-rearing these tend to predominate, as will be seen. The second and third parts of this chapter discuss positive and negative sanctions respectively. A final section provides some of the rationale behind the preference for the diffuse type of sanction in this context.

General methods

Environment and atmosphere

It is considered of the utmost importance that a secure and pleasant atmosphere be created for the business of child-rearing. The great emphasis on maintaining this congenial environment probably goes a long way towards explaining why Western observers regard Japanese children as indulged, for it is the aim at all times to avoid direct confrontation leading to bad feeling. Relations established at this time are considered to be the primary foundations of basic trust in other human beings, and trust and goodwill are essential if compliancy with authority is to be achieved in a child.[2] Manuals advise that parents should first of all take care to maintain a composed mood of enjoyment with their children, and specific aspects of the environment suggested recently are the providing of good music for them to hear and nice pictures for them to look at.[3]

In a recent study comparing maternal expectations for mastery of skills in Japan and the United States, the authors concluded that the expectations are expressed in quite different ways in the two countries. While the United States mothers use an 'environmental press', perhaps involving contingent rewards and direct instruction, the Japanese mothers are 'more likely to encourage the child to acquire desired behaviour by creating a climate of expectations and by fostering close emotional ties and a sense of responsibility to the family.[4] The promotion text of a card game setting out important values of Japanese society summarises the idea when it claims, 'while playing happily the children assimilate the necessary habits of daily life'.

The creation of this atmosphere begins before a child is even born since it is thought that the behaviour and feelings of the pregnant woman affect the child's health, character and abilities in later life. The mother is thus expected to provide a 'healthful environment' for the foetus by being nice to others, being industrious, and avoiding stressful experiences. Neighbours and other people surrounding the pregnant mother are expected to help her to maintain her physical and mental well-being.[5] The maintenance of this secure atmosphere is also the basic reason why in the early weeks and months after a baby is born it is kept as far as possible within the confines of the home, where it is rarely left to cry but enjoys a good deal of physical contact with its mother and other caretakers.

Breast-feeding used to be the norm, and until the end of the Second World War a baby used to sleep with its mother and be carried around on her back during a large part of her waking hours. Influence from the United States led to a great increase in the number of bottle-fed babies, separation of bedding due to propaganda about the danger of suffocation, and a vogue for the use of prams and push-chairs. The concern with the child's developing emotions continued, however, and recently there has been much concern, apparently again under Western influence, about the importance of 'skinship', a word adopted in Japanese in this form although it is not in common usage in English. Now professionals are advocating a return to breast-feeding and a paediatrician who has been described as Japan's equivalent of Dr Spock, Dr Michio Matsuda, protested against the imitation of Western ways 'in total disregard of the experience and wisdom of "thousands of years" '.[6] Push-chairs and prams are seen often enough in Japan nowadays, but the mother or grandmother with a baby on her back is by no means uncommon, and many caretakers use this method of freeing their hands while taking care of a baby, or of lulling it off to sleep for a daytime nap. It is part of the concern with this congenial atmosphere which makes the Western practice of putting a baby into a cot in another room and leaving it to cry itself to sleep shocking to most Japanese mothers. As was mentioned in Chapter I, even if they use a cot, they keep it next to their own bed and rarely put the baby into it until they have lulled it carefully off to sleep first.

An American study comparing the behaviour of mothers and their three- to four-month-old babies in Japan and the United States emphasises again and again the greater bodily contact in the Japanese case and the way the Japanese mother communicates physically rather than verbally with her child.[7] This physical contact is reinforced in the bath, which, as has been pointed out, is a pleasurable activity involving more than just washing. At home one or more adults and children may bathe with a baby; in a public bath house the baby enjoys not only the physical contact with its adult caretaker, but also the admiration of other members of the community.

Through all this physical contact, and by careful observation, mothers and other caretakers try to anticipate the baby's needs and attend to them before it has a chance to get anxious. This is a principle which continues, and children, in return, learn to read their mothers' and other people's facial expressions and understand their reactions to good and bad behaviour without having anything put into words. This type of understanding was mentioned in the last chapter as a specific objective of child training, and the creation of a secure and pleasant environment, together with a good deal of physical contact, would seem to be an important early element of the development of this non-verbal communication. As a child gets old enough to understand it, a mother may use the withdrawal of physical comfort to make a specific point. For example, this is a common tactic to discourage an older child from crying. The mother will stand away and encourage the child to 'be strong'. The ideal of cheerfulness in a small child has already been emphasised, and this is associated with the success of the mother in creating a happy congenial atmosphere for its upbringing.

Example

In order to encourage a child to develop good behaviour, great advantage is taken of the inclination of small children to copy what they see going on around them. Manuals advise parents from the very early days of their children's lives to behave in an exemplary fashion, to avoid quarrels in front of the children, and generally to try and become excellent members of society. More specifically, they point out that if a parent uses proper speech and the appropriate polite expressions, the child will learn to use them too; if the parents show love and care, and provide security and safety for their children, their emotions will develop well; if the parents demonstrate the proper way to behave, the children will follow. 'The child is the parents' mirror' quotes one such pamphlet.[8]

These are high ideals, and there is bound to be a wide range of practice amongst parents in everyday life, but they are taken very seriously. Mothers, in particular, seem to achieve considerable success, both in creating a pleasant, enjoyable atmosphere for their children, and in setting them a good example in ways to behave. This is perhaps partly linked to the way children are made the centre of the home and the caretakers' lives, so that people adapt their own lifestyles to having children around. It is also no doubt associated with the importance attached to this aspect of child-rearing methods in general, and adults other than the parents and grandparents cooperate to set a good example to children in their own community. It thus has the advantage of regulating to some extent the behaviour of adults in public, as children are banned from very few spheres of social life. It is possible, of course, that parents are much more careful in this respect when they are in the public eye, since disapproval would no doubt accompany any other sort of behaviour, but within the families with which we became quite intimate during research the exemplary behaviour persisted right into the inner recesses of the home.

It could be argued that the presence of a foreign observer would affect the behaviour of parents even in their own homes, and I think that this is a valid criticism which has been made of research carried out by observers little known to their informants. However, I spent a great number of hours on many days during the course of my six months' research in the home of my assistant, who accorded us many of the privileges of members of the family, and she maintained a pleasant example to her children throughout that time. Of course, she may be unusual, but we also had neighbours with small children the other side of a very thin wall from us, and I think it would be true to say that I never heard the mother raise her voice, either to an often quite miserable baby or to her mischievous four-year-old. Indeed, Japanese accommodation is often as close as this to neighbours, which may be an important influence in this respect. Certainly the maintenance of a pleasant disposition seemed quite definitely to be the rule, which could hardly be said to be the case in England, though I know less of the United States in this respect. This is not to say that children are never punished, as will be seen in subsequent sections, merely that mothers seem to take very seriously the importance of remaining congenial and setting a good example to their children. Other observers have noted the way in which children learn many adult skills through observation and imitation rather than by direct instruction, and parents are also described as engaging in 'ceaseless, patient demonstration' for children to imitate.[9] Many parents also emphasise the importance of saying themselves the greetings and ritual phrases they expect their children to learn, putting into practice the manners they explain they should observe, and carrying out the rites of cleanliness and order they hope to impart to their children. With regard to moral values, they explain to children old enough to understand the rationale behind the positive behaviour they carry out themselves and the negative behaviour they discourage or disapprove of in others so that, again, the children learn, by example, what are the important values of their own communities.

The role of the television should be mentioned here again, for small children spend many hours in front of the screen and there are many programmes designed to help with their upbringing. On these, too, the compères adopt the pleasant manner caretakers afford their charges, and create by means of cheerful music, bright decorations and lively characters an atmosphere of fun and enjoyment. They also devote much time to having their characters carry out their activities in the proper way, or perhaps having them make mistakes and be instructed about where they went wrong, so that they can demonstrate at last that they have learned when and how to say sorry, thank you, good morning, and so on. Much of the material covered in the last chapter is systematically demonstrated in these television programmes, which no doubt aids mothers greatly in setting a good example to their young children. It should also be noted, however, that there is a lot of violence on Japanese television which is often watched by children, although it is not necessarily reproduced in their behaviour.

Older children, too, are encouraged to set a good example to younger ones, and are made to feel important that they are able to do this. This practice has the added desirable effect of regulating the behaviour of the other children, some of whom, especially girls, take such a role very seriously. Thus, as toddlers begin to follow their older brothers and sisters into the neighbourhood, the older children are encouraged to take responsibility for the little ones, setting them a good example and providing instruction in the proper way to behave. It is not uncommon for a relationship of this sort to exist for a while between two unrelated children in a neighbourhood. My assistant found a neighbour's seven-year-old more punctilious about training her three-year-old daughter than she was herself, and the older obviously took great pride in this achievement. Since most children in the families of the interview sample did play in the neighbourhood, this may well form an important complement to the example set by parents in the early stages of experience in the outside world.

Repetition

Another important element of child training emphasised in the manuals is repetition. The gist of the advice is that, for daily customs, mothers should take care to be quite determined in their methodical repetition of behaviour patterns. Indeed, we have already come across this type of advice in the discussion of toilet training in the last chapter, when it was reported that the public health nurse advised that the same person should take my son to the same place at the same times each day in order to train him to use his potty. The repetition each time of onomatopoeic phrases for the elimination involved ensures that these words are early learned and recognised. The same principle applies to the other customs associated with cleanliness and order. Mothers should put their children through the same motions at each meal, and at each entry into the house, each time they take a bath, and each time they get dressed or undressed. As Benedict wrote, 'It is the habit that is taught, not just the rules . . . the movements are performed over and over literally under the hands of grown-ups until they are automatic'.[10] Norbeck and Norbeck noted the same use of repetition in the teaching of manners: 'Once the use of chopsticks is habitual, the mother repeatedly admonishes against dropping food, . . . the tone of voice is soft but instruction is insistent and unfailing'.[11]

This does in practice seem to be a very common method used in child training. Mothers or other caretakers repeat over and over again the phrases they want their children to learn, without making undue fuss if the child fails to copy. Rather than telling the child what to say and waiting for him or her to say it, they just say the phrase for them and many a time the child will join in quite happily. In the case of movements, like bowing or removing shoes, or activities such as washing or using chopsticks, the mother puts the child through the motions regularly and at the appropriate time, until the child gradually learns to do the things, by force of habit, for itself. Perhaps because the mother is involved so much in the early stages, there is sometimes a problem for her to retreat, which may explain to some extent the concern as an objective of *shitsuke* with children doing things for themselves.

The use of repetition is particularly noticeable in the passing on of language to small children. As Benedict pointed out, 'They do not leave the baby's acquiring of language to chance imitation'.[12] Rather, a whole series of baby words are used and used again, time after time, until the baby responds by saying the words itself. Many of the words are actually a sound repeated twice themselves, for example:

umauma food	*poppo* train	*tete* hand	*kukku* shoe
niannian cat	*uanuan* dog	*būbū* car	*totto* fish *mōmō* cow

When such an object is in view, adults will point it out to the child, giving its name in this baby talk, and repeating it over and over again. This type of repetition of simple words for babies who are just beginning to speak is apparently quite common in many languages, but in the amount of repetition, often by several adults at once, Japan must take a leading place. Nor is it simply first words. As the child develops the ability to pronounce longer phrases, these too are repeated as thought appropriate by the surrounding adults in the neighbourhood and elsewhere. Anyone meeting a baby may join in with this game and many people do. There are people in Japan, as in the West, who spurn baby-talk as silly and time-wasting, but they still go in for repetition, even if it is of words which the baby finds less easy to pronounce.

Greetings and other *aisatsu* are taught in this way too. As people accompanied by a baby or small child go about their business in the outside world, they are constantly pronouncing phrases appropriate to the situations in which they find themselves and, gradually, sure enough, the child joins in or copies the same phrases.

Again, television reinforces this method of training. Many of the programmes which present material designed for very small children are repeated daily, with many little parts of them being repeated each time, or being changed only slightly eventually to include a range of aspects of child training. The children learn the routine and the ditties, and they love to join in. These programmes often also repeat the phrases and other aspects of child-training that the mothers have been teaching, which gives a good indication of the universality of many important daily customs.

Explanation and solicitude

Once children begin to speak and comprehend what adults say to them, their caretakers start explaining the reasons behind the various things they are expected to do. This becomes particularly important from the age of about three years when children are thought to have developed the ability to understand explanations, although rationale behind prohibitions based on danger may be demonstrated before that time. If a toddler persists in approaching a hot fire, for example, the mother may gently draw the child's hand into a place close enough to feel the heat, so that the child becomes afraid to go any nearer. However, once the child attains the age of about three years, the explanations become more elaborate. They are often couched in the moral terms discussed in the previous chapter, so that a common phrase used is: 'how would you like it if another child did to you what you are doing to them?' A child is made to feel grown up, that it has now reached the age of rationality. For example, when it is encouraged to give in while playing with smaller children, it is emphasised that this is a sign that is is older and thereby able to understand, and the older it gets the more it will be able to understand, so that the principle continues in interaction between children of different ages. It is considered important at this stage for children to play in the neighbourhood so that they learn to deal with outside relationships.

Less high-minded explanations are also used which may involve promise of reward or threat of punishment or disapproval, as will be discussed in more detail shortly, but the reason for mentioning explanation as a method at this stage is the place accorded this by mothers describing their approaches to child-rearing. When asked about punishments or other specific deterrents to bad behaviour, mothers frequently begin their reply by saying that they try to avoid strong negative sanctions by 'causing their child to understand' the reason why they should not do such a thing. In the same way, they state often that they prefer to explain why a thing should be done rather than offer rewards so that the child only does something for what it will receive in return. It is a common sight in Japan to see a mother bending down to a small child who seems set on some course of action, patiently speaking in a firm but pleasant voice to bring the child round to her way of thinking on the subject. Sometimes such solicitude fails, but it is also by no means rare to see the child agree in the end and comply with the mother's wishes.

Other writers have commented on the importance of explanation in child-rearing methods in Japan, and Befu refers to national opinion surveys in which a majority of respondents prefer 'explaining thoroughly the reason why a child must do what he is told to do' to other methods such as bribes or mild threats.[13] Befu goes on to compare the approach of Japanese and American mothers, noting that the former uses solicitude rather than authority, which the latter might use, pleading with and begging a difficult child to do as he is told, rather than standing firm and meting out punishment if necessary, which he sees as more likely behaviour in the latter case. He adds that an American mother would look ridiculous to bystanders if she begged and pleaded with a three-to-five-year-old, whereas a Japanese mother who took an authoritarian approach would be regarded as lacking in human feeling.[14]

In fact, I think that recent Western influence has altered this slightly and many mothers complained to me that their own mothers or mothers-in-law were too soft with children, who needed to be treated more strictly, as they understand to be the case in Europe. Television programmes sometimes include interviews with European mothers and experts on child-rearing with the aim of learning from them about the stricter approach. However, the emphasis on explanation as a first method of gaining compliance still seems to be very strong, and it is perhaps when this method fails that the authoritative tone is thought to be required. It should also be mentioned here that mothers sometimes point out that they would not punish a child until they were sure that the child understood what it had done wrong.[15]

Positive sanctions

Praise

It was noted in the previous chapter that some mothers denied they used praise as a method of training their children, and the answers to the question 'what do you praise your child for?' seemed to suggest that the child should do a little more than is normally expected before praise is forthcoming. Nor is praise mentioned very much in the manuals as an important aspect of training. Yet words of praise to small children abound in the chatter which surrounds groups of adults with one or more small children in their company. For even the barest greeting a child is called 'clever' or 'good boy/girl' and it seems that a child going about in the world is often praised for little accomplishments or comments. The Norbecks, writing about child training in rural Japan some twenty-five years ago, pointed to praise and approving pats on the top of the head as a positive sanction used particularly by grandparents, and Lanham, working in the 1960s, also mentioned this as a means of training, although she qualified her remarks by pointing out that a child who gets too vain will become the subject of ridicule.[16]

It seems possible, though this is something that has occurred to me since our return and therefore not investigated directly in the field, that it is more the role of outsiders to praise small children for their conformity with normal expectations of behaviour than that of the mother or other caretaker who is responsible for their training. Since the view seems to be strongly held that the child is a white sheet and the colours it displays are those imbued by its caretakers, it would be almost like praising herself if a mother praised her child for doing only what is expected. If it steps beyond those bounds, then she may legitimately praise it, but otherwise it would seem to be up to outsiders, particularly neighbours, but perhaps even only as far outside as grandparents, to comment on the success of her training. This theory would fit in with the general practice in polite language of humbling oneself and one's own family in coversation with others, to whom one accords deferential phrases of respect. It would also provide for the child another boundary between the inside members of its own household and people of the outside world.

Reward and reciprocity

The Japanese word for 'reward' (*gohōbi*) has the same base character as that for 'to praise' (*homeru*), and perhaps for this reason, it was also denied by many mothers as a means of training when the word was used directly. However, methods which would certainly be classed in English as using rewards were commonly employed by mothers, who also explained in detail the sort of occasion on which they found them particularly effective. For example, mothers who said specifically that they would not use rewards went on to describe how they would buy a child books if it was good at the dentist, sweets if it was good when they were out, and juice if it was good while its mother was working. Some such practices might even be termed bribes in English since they were evidently used to persuade a child to conform: one mother said she promised to make her children banana juice or ice cream if they settled down quietly to have a rest; another to produce ice cream if a child ate up all its rice; another that she promised nice things if a child accompanied her to a place where it was reluctant to go; yet another gave her daughter sweets if she kept quiet while her baby sister was sleeping.

Occasionally mothers did term this type of behaviour use of reward, especially if it was a more momentous occasion, such as sleeping alone for the first time, going unaided to the toilet, or starting kindergarten happily, but there was also some reluctance expressed for encouraging a child to do something only for the sake of what it would receive, and failing, as the Norbecks put it, 'to teach that proper behaviour is desireable for its own sake'.[17]

It seems that, rather, the method is used partly to inculcate in a child the principles of reciprocity. Many of the examples already cited are specific exchanges of one thing for another, and one mother I interviewed said quite clearly that she only used the method of reward if it was an exchange for something specific such as help or an errand. In American terminology, it is the equivalent of 'doing a deal'. As the children grow to the stage of understanding money, they may be given pocket money for specific tasks such as these, and some mothers mentioned this practice in the context of discussions about the rewarding of good behaviour so it seems to be directly comparable. For example, some gave pocket money for help in the house, for taking messages to other houses, or to older children for taking care of the younger ones for a period. Again, however, most of the occasions mentioned seem to involve just a little more than the normal good behaviour expected in the course of everyday life, and for these, the children receive just a little more than their normal quota of benevolence from adults.

There is also an element of convenience involved here, and one couple who were engaged in farm work were quite explicit about how they used promises of ice cream to keep children amused while they carried out their tasks for the day. It is all very well for mothers and grandmothers who devote themselves full time to child care, to maintain high ideals in the methods they use, but where economic necessity or mothers who prefer to work prevent the release of a member of the family for this purpose, there is no doubting the advantages of such inducements to co-operation. In the country community, where most of the mothers worked outside the home as well as having small children, many respondents were quite categorical in their denial of the use of rewards, although the local shop appeared to be doing a roaring trade in sweets and ice creams. In this sense it might have been better to have categorised the use of such devices as aspects of solicitude and persuasion as discussed above.

The same principles are put into operation when children are taken by adults on trains or in other public places, where they might be annoying people, and a mother producing a large selection of sweets from her handbag is no rare sight in such situations. Explanation is fine if it has the desired effect, but there is no harm in making contingency plans if it would be too embarrassing were such methods to fail. One of the most common arguments used in explanations is that things should not be done that would annoy or put to trouble other people, but perhaps it takes a while for a child to realise the importance accorded this maxim.

Negative sanctions

Punishment

The most organised negative sanctions are specific punishments, three types of which are used widely in Japan, albeit somewhat sparingly. The first is corporal punishment, the most common method being a smack. This is not often administered in public, but most of the interview respondents said that they did smack their children from time to time if they refused to listen, or if they were particularly naughty. Some pointed out that the smacks were merely rather light taps, or loudly administered rather than painfully, and those that I witnessed were given with a clear explanation of the reason why. Some mothers use this method of punishment before the child is old enough to understand explanation, perhaps to ward a toddler away from danger, and then stop smacking from the age of three. Others continue to use the method until the child starts school, or a little later. Another form of light corporal punishment mentioned was pinching, on the arm or leg usually, and the formation of the fingers into a scissor-shape is used to warn a child that if it doesn't behave such a punishment will be forthcoming.

More severe methods of corporal punishment are used occasionally and their existence as a possibility is probably a powerful deterrent to bad behaviour. The well-known one which has shocked several Western writers into describing it in some detail is *moxa cautery*, or the burning of a little incense on the skin. As mentioned in Chapter I, this is described as a cure, rather than a punishment, and it may be administered by a specialist outsider the first time, a little of the substance being taken home for further treatment. It is said to be extremely painful, however, and parents explained that getting the powder out is enough to ensure conformity immediately, once a child has experienced it. Not many people mentioned this, however, and it is likely that its use is declining. A modern substitute for such a method may be the burning of skin with a cigarette lighter, which I did see one father threaten, although no one gave this as an example of punishment used. One of two families did say that they used the wooden *kendō* sword if severe punishment was necessary, but, again, this seemed to be something of a last resort.

The second specific type of punishment used occasionally is the isolation of a child in a dark cupboard or storehouse. This is usually for a short period of time, one mother said twenty minutes or so, until the child says sorry for what it has done wrong. One father said that he wouldn't use this method because he was still afraid of the dark himself after having experienced this form of punishment as a child. His wife said that instead she ignores the child and refuses to play with him, which suggests that the method is really an extreme form of the withdrawal of the usual benevolence accorded children. In three-generation families mothers said that they found the method rather ineffective since the grandparents would soon feel sorry for the child and let it out, and a mother in a nuclear family said the same about her husband. Nevertheless, the method exists as a well-known possible punishment, and as such is, again, said to be a deterrent for bad behaviour.

The third type of punishment makes use of the same principle of withdrawal of benevolence and separation from the 'inside group', which, as Hara and Wagatsuma have pointed out, is found in different forms all over Japan.[18] This time the child is put out of the house, particularly at night. One mother who used this method successfully said that she had done it only once, but that she had left her two boys of six and seven out for one whole night and the duration of four mealtimes, until they agreed to promise not to do what they had done again. This case involved the removal of money from her purse, and both boys denied having done the deed, each blaming the other, so she was concerned to teach them that both stealing and lying were wrongs worthy of such a punishment. She added that since they were hungry while they thought about the situation they would surely remember it, and since neither boy had stolen or lied to her during the subsequent period of some years, she thought it had been successful. She admitted to having had little rest that night herself, but she commented that since it was July, at least they were not cold, and she was convinced that the punishment had been worth the disquiet it caused. Again, the principle is seen of having so severe a punishment that it is unnecessary to put it often into practice.

Other parents reported success with this method, though none seemed to have been so severe. Once case involved the tying of a little girl to a tree in front of the house, but this was only for an hour in the middle of the day, after which the girl was prepared to apologise. In other cases, too, the period was soon curtailed by the willingness of the child alone outside at night to apologise. Some parents were less successful, since they felt sorry for the child before that stage was reached and so brought them back inside. At the other extreme, the child sometimes seems to outwit the parents by going off somewhere, or, in one case, by rushing in while his mother was taking rubbish out and turning the tables by locking his mother out.

The Vogels, who have also described this form of punishment, commented that in the United States a child would be more likely to be kept in, and they relate this to the greater dependency fostered in Japanese children as opposed to the independence in American ones.[19] However, it seemed to be the case, from my experience, that children are allowed to play outside the house in Japan as early as if not earlier than they are in some Western countries, where there seems to be less willingness to rely on neighbours and other adults to be benevolent to them. There is also the possibility of confining a child to a cupboard or outhouse, if the method of putting outside is thought better avoided. It seems that the important point in both cases is that the child is being ostracised by the people from whom it can normally expect benevolence; it is being separated from the 'inside group' to which it belongs. Such a sanction is also used in villages, when one family persistently and apparently purposely incurs the disapproval of neighbours, who decide eventually to ostracise all the members of the recalcitrant family for a specific period of time. Again, it is a severe form of punishment which is rarely put into practice, but its existence is apparently an effective deterrent to uncooperative behaviour. In the case of putting a child out of the house it does again confirm the inside/outside boundary, as may the locking-in of a child if it is put into an outhouse or storeroom which is actually outside the main part of the home.

Threats and supernatural sanctions

It is evident that knowledge of the existence of severe forms of punishment for small children makes the threat of their use an effective sanction and this method is also used in a number of other ways. Some are quite trivial threats such as the withdrawal of objects discussed in the section on rewards, like sweets and ice cream, or the denial of privileges like being taken swimming, shopping or to play in the park. Occasionally the wrath of the child's father may be threatened, but unknown outsiders may also be referred to in order to frighten a child into conforming, and some mention policemen in this respect. Again playing on a child's fear, another mother said that she warns an injection will be necessary if teeth are not cleaned regularly. Yet another family reported that they tell a naughty child that the grandmother will put her in a bag, take her somewhere she doesn't know and leave her there.

Making use of a similar technique of frightening the child, a number of supernatural sanctions are drawn upon, typically demons, ghosts and unpleasant deities. My assistant noted that her three-year-old daughter was particularly affected by pictures of demons shown on television at *setsubun*, a festival day when rites are performed to exorcise the home from demons, and she began to tell her that demons eat naughty girls. The mention of such demons ensured instant compliance. Similar fears are reported by Yamamoto for the north-east of Japan, and many informants reported success with the threat of ghosts: the Maretzkis, writing about Okinawa, described an incident they witnessed where a neighbour was employed to dress up as a ghost to frighten a persistently naughty boy.[20] In Kurotsuchi the presence of a shrine to the deity of thunder and lightning made this a convenient character to invoke, but he was also mentioned by respondents in Tateyama, so he was obviously more widely feared. One mother said that she told the child that this deity would send lightning to take away her tummy button if she was naughty. Gods in general are said to be able to see good and bad behaviour so that one should be careful to behave even when no one else was watching.

In general, the encouragement of fear, and eventually courage, seems to be quite an important part of child training. The word for 'danger' (*abunai*) is used a great deal by adults with small children, as I learned first of all by having to translate it endlessly before my own children could understand any Japanese. I noticed then that in

English we would be much more likely to use the positive phrase 'be careful' than the negative one 'that's dangerous'. In the country, some old people went further, especially at night, and pointed down dark alleyways suggesting that there might be a ghost or a big dog lurking there, so that the child should remain close to the safety of the adult's side.

The Vogels noted this form of behaviour in their work with families in Tokyo, and pointed out that the mother comforts and protects the child against frightening things, but does not deny that they are frightening. This they contrast with the American case where they say that mothers would be more likely to reassure a child with the words 'don't be afraid', so that again the Japanese mother is encouraging dependence rather than independence.[21] Some mothers in Kurotsuchi said that they were reluctant to mention ghosts to their children because they were frightened of them themselves, which does seem to support the idea that the mother should be in a position to protect.

This example illustrates the effectiveness of the inculcation of fear in children, when it is still evident in the adults themselves. Another common fear is that of being alone in a deserted mountainous area. Once when I lost my way in the car at dusk, trying to find a mountain inn, I asked the way in a seaside resort a few miles from my destination, only to be greeted with looks of horror and disbelief from a group of full-grown men that I should be setting off into the mountains when night was coming on. They first suggested that I should put up in a local hotel until the morning, but when I explained that I had left all my luggage, as well as my companions, at the inn in the mountains, they managed to find a taxi driver who was returning home that way to guide me to a crossroads where I would be sure to find my way. The fact that two small children were sitting in the car may have influenced their reaction, but I have come across this fear of uninhabited countryside in other adults even in broad daylight.

The development of fear seems to be associated always with outsiders and the outside of the house, and it is perhaps an important contrast with the safety and indulgence of the inside, which has also been carefully fostered. Indeed, one of the earliest uses of the word *abunai* (danger) may be when a crawling baby approaches the outside door, since there is usually quite a steep drop down to the place where shoes are left. Even as the child learns to negotiate the drop and put on its own shoes, it is still potentially dangerous for it to stray outside alone. Later, threats of punishment and supernatural retribution are very often attributed to outsiders, as Befu has pointed out.[22]

Courage was a quality mentioned in the section on aspirations as especially desirable in boys, and some games for slightly older children involve creating frightening situations so that courage may be tested. A popular activity at summer camps and when young school children stay away from home for the night is an expedition in the darkness, during which adults dress up as ghosts and jump out on groups of children as they go by. The youngsters cluster together for comfort and there seems to be an emphasis here on the safety of co-operating with the group. Horrible monsters are popular toys, especially amongst boys, and television programmes reinforce this theme of co-operation when men fail to conquer the monsters alone, but overcome them when they join forces. Stories told to small children also often involve rather frightening supernatural beings, such as demons and monsters, but a central character who conforms with the moral code is usually able to outwit them, which is further indirect use of supernatural sanctions as a training method.

Ridicule

Another sanction commonly used is to laugh at a child who is acting up, or suggest that other people will find him or her ridiculous. A particularly cutting comment is that a baby will laugh, although a variety of friends and admired adults may be suggestd as likely to scorn silly behaviour of one sort or another. With tiny children this method is applied if they wet their pants, or if they cry for no good reason, and the range of behaviour likely to induce scorn enlarges as the child grows older. Particularly for crying, the child is dubbed *okashii,* which means strange, peculiar or laughable, unlike everyone else, the opposite of the ideal quality of ordinary or average, which was discussed in the last chapter. Adults describe the way they were afraid, as children, of having no friends if they were different, so that they tried to behave in the same way as their companions. Children everywhere are concerned about doing the right thing, wearing the right clothes, having the right equipment etc., but this is especially emphasised in Japan, where ridicule of unusual behaviour is actually encouraged. Groups of youngsters rally round to point and jeer at a child who fails to conform, which provided an interesting phenomenon for my older son whose English background prepared him rather to enjoy making people laugh.

This fear of ridicule continues into adult life, forming an important aspect of the pressure to conform found in Japanese society more generally. This early practice seems to lie behind the concern of most Japanese to be accepted as a regular member of the group or groups to which they belong. Hara and Wagatsuma note that people might well be proud that, despite being poor, at least they are not laughed at.[23] It is part of the wider fear of ostracism from the group, though in this sense it is the community rather than the family which is concerned, since ridicule brought on one member tends to reflect badly on the whole family, which provides another strong disincentive against incurring it.

The Norbecks noted that, as a child matures, disciplinary measures tend increasingly away from physical punishment and more towards censure designed to make the child feel ashamed,[24] and this is borne out by my own work. The earliest form of punishment is a simple smack, but as a child becomes able to understand them, threats of isolation, ridicule and ostracism become more common. At first the agents of punishment are within the home, when the child is learning to establish its own identity, but gradually threats are attributed to outsiders, emphasising the increasingly important distinction between the inside and outside of the house or family unit. This is reinforced by the use of punishments which temporarily isolate the child from this unit.

As the child develops further, however, it becomes aware of the neighbourhood or other wider community to which it belongs, and threats of ridicule are couched in terms of being ostracised by members of this new larger group. Lanham suggests that this threat that people will laugh at you or your family encourages withdrawal within the kinship group,[25] but I think that, while it continues to distinguish the family group from the outside, it represents rather a new stage of awareness of belonging and conforming to a wider group. The importance of general co-operation within this wider group was mentioned briefly in the section above on fear. An older child begins to participate in community groups such as the children's group, and, later, the youth group, but for the pre-school child first formal co-operation is learned in the kindergarten or day nursery, the subject matter of the next chapter.

Limitations to punishment and scolding

It should be emphasised that despite this range of negative sanctions available for use, most informants mentioned at least one or two that they would not use at all, usually explaining that they wanted their child to behave well for its own sake, rather than because of some outside force compelling them. Others claim not to use organised positive sanctions such as rewards for the same reasons. Hara reports that Japanese believe too much scolding and prohibition before a child can fully understand what adults say hinders the development of their basic trust in other people, thereby making it difficult in adulthood to maintain smooth and harmonious relations with co-workers, friends and business acquaintances.[26] Another writer, DeVos, points out that excessive scolding is linked to unsuccessful results, and that children are thought to develop negative attitudes or become soured if they are punished with severity. He notes that mothers are constantly self-conscious about the possible influence of their behaviour on future development and avoid direct refusal of demands by ignoring them or distracting a child from them.[27] It is often considered better to give in to a child who insists on some action the mother has tried to discourage rather than create bad feeling by refusing it outright.

This was illustrated on one occasion when I was visiting a Japanese family at the time when the daughter was being put to bed. I had taken a new tape to the house which was being played on the family stereo equipment, but the child wanted to listen to her own tape as she settled down to sleep. The family stereo machine was in the section of the room in which she was being settled, so my tape was transferred to a portable machine, which was placed outside the sliding doors which separated her area from that where we were sitting, and her tape was put into the family machine, now closed into her sleeping area. This did not quiet her crying, however, and after various attempts to soothe her it emerged that she wanted to listen to her own tape on the portable machine so that ours would need to be removed altogether. It seemed to me that a Western reaction would have been to insist that the child use the machine in her own area so that the adult activities could continue, but, in the end, this family took off the tape that we were listening to so that their daughter could be appeased. The mother apologised, pointing out that a crying child always wins.

It might be thought that this attitude is changing, since parents claim to seek to enforce greater discipline, and complain about the laxity and lack of discipline displayed by grandparents. Also, Inoguchi claims that while the making of 'one portion' of a person was the original meaning of *shitsuke*, the inclusion of punishment and restraint in the concept came afterwards.[28] However, this type of complaint actually seems to be rather traditional since there is a saying that a child brought up by grandparents is cheap goods (because it is spoilt).[29] My assistant, who has had considerable experience abroad and must be among the most modern Japanese mothers, was visibly shocked by her own sister-in-law who, after having lived in Greece some years with her children, was quite harsh with them in enforcing her own way. It seems, still, that most mothers prefer where possible to make as much use as they can of the positive diffuse rearing methods outlined at the beginning of this chapter, avoiding outright disputes and differences and concentrating instead on compliance and harmony in their relationships with their children.

It will be seen subsequently that these principles apply again in wider relationships, and indeed, continue into adult life. It has been commented that even the Japanese legal system relies much more heavily on mediation and conciliation than on litigation and the application of universally applicable principles, as in the case of Western legal systems. In general, in the resolution of disputes, human elements are considered in individual cases, and mutual trust, sincerity and good faith are emphasised over legalistic adherence to principle.[30] This approach evidently begins at a very early stage.

Notes

1 Radcliffe Brown 1952: chapter XI.
2 Hara 1980: 19.
3 *Yōji no Kokoroe*: 5; Ibuka 1976.
4 Hess *et al.* 1980: 269.
5 Hara 1980: 1; cf. Norbeck & Norbeck 1956: 652 for an example of specific dietary restrictions. These ideas would appear to be among the underlying assumptions of the recent novel by Ishiguro Kazuo, *A Pale View of the Hills,* unfortunately probably quite lost on the average English reader for whose benefit it was presumably published (in Penguin).
6 Lebra 1976: 138; Matsuda 1973: 3–4; cf. Hirai 1977.
7 Caudill & Weinstein 1974: 225–76.
8 New Morals 1981: 21; cf. *Yōji no Kokoroe*: 6; Ibuka 1976; *Mama Wakatte ne*; this aspect of training was also observed by Thunberg in eighteenth-century Japan (Moloney 1962: 216).
9 Smith 1962: 193; cf. Maretzki & Maretzki 1963: 144.
10 Benedict 1977: 197.
11 Norbeck & Norbeck 1956: 659.
12 Benedict 1977: 181.
13 Befu 1971: 157; cf. Lanham 1966: 327.
14 *Ibid.* 156–7.
15 Cf. Lanham 1966: 327.
16 Norbeck & Norbeck 1956: 661–2; Lanham 1966: 330.
17 *Ibid.* p. 662.
18 Hara & Wagatsuma 1974:67.
19 Vogel & Vogel 1961: 165.
20 Maretzki & Maretzki 1963: 139. Similar techniques are reported by Yoshiko Yamamoto (1978: 121ff) for north-east Japan, by Raum (1940: 213) for the Chaga, and by Levy (1973: 448) for the Tahitians.
21 Vogel & Vogel 1961: 163.
22 Befu 1971: 158.
23 Hara & Wagatsuma 1974: 77.
24 Norbeck & Norbeck 1956: 661.
25 Lanham 1966: 332.
26 Hara 1980: 11.
27 Devos 1973: 88; cf. Lanham 1966: 328.
28 Inoguchi 1962: 220.
29 Hara & Wagatsuma 1974: 156.
30 Koschmann 1974: 100.

Chapter Five

The kindergarten and day nursery: formal entry into a social world

The importance of the role of the kindergarten or day nursery in the pre-school period has already been outlined in Chapter II, where it was pointed out that the chief aim is to supplement home education, 'to develop the minds and health of the children' and to introduce them to group life in preparation for entry into primary school. The day nursery has the additional purpose of providing care for the children of working mothers. At these establishments *shitsuke* is continued, with the particular new aspect of training in peer inter-action and co-operation within the larger group, without which parents feel that their children would become selfish and over-indul-ged. Some of the history of kindergartens and day nurseries was also covered in Chapter II, as was the range of types of such institutions. In Chapter I some idea was given about the influence that kindergar-ten teachers have over home life, once children enter this public system. The concern of this chapter will be to describe the content of kindergarten or nursery education, particularly with reference to the establishments where research was conducted, and to follow through some of the principles of child training already established in their more formal context.

The first section summarises the nationally prescribed aims and standards for kindergartens and nurseries, together with their recommended categories of study, and looks at some of the parents' aspirations for their own children's development through kinder-garten.

In the second section some detail is provided about the institutions where research was carried out so that the reader may have an idea of the degree to which these are representative. The common features of day nurseries and kindergartens will then be described in sections on the layout of the rooms, the activities engaged in, and the ways in which children participate in the organisation of kindergarten life. There will then be some analysis of the principles involved in institutional training, comparing those which coincide with home training and outlining those which emerge as new methods applicable to group interaction. It should be evident that ethical standards continue and reinforce the values which have been taught before a child enters such a group.

National standards and parental aspirations

Anyone who wishes to establish a kindergarten or day nursery must get official authorisation from the prefectural authorities and must operate it in accordance with various regulations and standards specified in national laws. These apply to curriculum, personnel and their qualifications, number of days' operation a year, and number of hours a day, facilities and equipment. There are rules about the amount of space and the number of lavatories per child, for example, but it is also stipulated that each kindergarten should have slides, swings, sand pits, building blocks, picture books, pianos or organs and other musical instruments, as well as desks, chairs and blackboards.[1] The day nursery must provide daily examinations of the health of the children including complexion, temperature, skin and state of cleanliness, to be carried out on the arrival before the guardian leaves. The course of study for kindergartens is prescribed by the Ministry of Education and includes 137 possible activities in six categories, namely health, society, nature, language, musical rhythm and art. Day nurseries should follow the standards for kindergarten curriculum for the children of the same age, and rather fewer, but similar items for younger children. One class in a kindergarten should be composed 'as a rule' of not more than forty children, and in a day nursery there should be one adult for every three babies under one year, for every six infants under three, for every twenty from three to four, and for every thirty for children of four and over.[2]

The aims and objectives of pre-school education are laid out, for kindergartens in articles 77 and 78 of the School Education Law, and for day nurseries in article 39 of the Child Welfare Law. For kindergartens, the chief aim is 'to bring up young children and develop their minds and bodies by providing a suitable environment for them', and more specific objectives include 'cultivating everyday habits necessary for a sound, safe and happy life', to make children 'experience group-life and cultivate a willingness to take part in it as well as the germ of the spirit of co-operation and self-reliance', 'right understanding' and 'the right attitude to the surrounding social life', 'right use of language' and the 'cultivation of the children's own creative expression through music, play, drawing and other means'. The aims of the day nursery are similar, but include that of 'bringing up babies and children who lack their upbringing at their homes', and extra objectives such as 'stabilising children's emotion', and the cultivating of 'rich sentiment' and 'embryos of morality'.[3]

Parental aspirations for children entering kindergarten, as declared in the forms of application for places at Shirayuri private kindergarten, are mostly congruent with the national aims. One actually mentioned the 'development of mind and body' through contact with other children, but many more made reference to becoming used to group life, learning to play with other children, and becoming a 'social person'. The ideals of co-operation and harmony were mentioned too, as were general matters of manners and training (*shitsuke*). More specific detailed aims such as learning to speak properly, to eat without fuss, and to go to the toilet alone were also included. Aspects of moral development discussed in Chapter III, such as kindness, perseverence and thought for others, also sometimes appeared here as did the cultivation of independence and personal character. A word which recurred in parental aspirations, both here and in a section on home educational aims, was *nobinobi,* which means 'carefree' or 'a feeling of ease', which seems to be gained through an early understanding of how to interact with others so that this becomes as natural as possible, and the child feels free to play without worrying about petty concerns. Some parents

121

also gave the kindergarten a written licence to scold or punish their child if it misbehaved. Finally, hopes about 'creative expression' were usually couched in the context of the speciality of this kindergarten, namely musical abilities and appreciation.

Specific institutions studied

Shirayuri Kindergarten was the institution to which we were attached during five of the six months of our stay in Japan for this research. We stayed in accommodation loaned to us by the headmistress and owner, who was also our neighbour; my son attended as a regular pupil so that I was a member of the PTA; and our nanny gave periodic English classes, which led to informal visits from other teachers and some of her pupils, who were also mothers of children there. These close associations made possible some valuable daily interaction providing an insight into the workings of an institution such as this which would not otherwise easily have been accessible to us. The establishment was somewhat singular, however, since it was the only private kindergarten in Tateyama and therefore catered for the upper-income bracket of families which tended to have a higher than average motivation for their children's achievements. It specialised in the teaching of English and music, reflecting the accomplishments of the headmistress. She had spent some years in California and brought an approach to pre-school education which was influenced by this experience. This did not result in extreme Westernisation, however, since in some ways she seemed to have reacted to her understanding of the United States by emphasising Japanese values. Her declared aim was to equip children for upper-class life in Japan by training in proper manners and attitudes and the development of appreciation and sensitivity. The former she set out to achieve through discipline, and the latter by the provision of spacious and attractive surroundings for free play, filled with the strains of classical music from a loudspeaker over the office.

The teachers she chose for their qualities of character rather than for their teaching techniques in which she claimed she could and subsequently did train them if they were the right sort of people. She expected them to be advised by her on their own manners and style of dress, and work from 7 a.m. to 6 or 7 p.m., six days a week, sometimes with extra duties on Sundays. She strove for excellence and strict discipline in teachers and pupils alike, operating on the principle that a child under proper guidance is capable of developing any talents at all.

There are many private kindergartens in Japan, particularly in urban areas, often with their own equally high ideals and particular specialities, so that it was appropriate to observe such an institution in detail. However, there are also a large number of public kindergartens whose aims are less lofty though still in keeping with national standards. I therefore spent considerable time in Tateyama making detailed observations in some of these, to offset the particular experience gained at Shirayuri. One of the ways in which kindergartens cultivate 'the right attitude to the surrounding social life' is by adapting to local circumstances, so I chose institutions in three rather different parts of Tateyama and the surrounding district.

One of these was Tateyama Kindergarten, which was set in the heart of the urban district. I also spent slightly less time at another, larger kindergarten in the city centre, which had benefited from being the nearest to the City Hall and therefore recipient of the latest equipment which was likely to impress visiting dignitaries. In each of these, the numbers were very large, nearly four-hundred in the first and five-hundred in the second, the children being divided by age group into classes of between thirty and forty, who take it in turn to make use of ample common facilities such as playgrounds and sand-pits. The same teacher stays with a class for each of the two years spent there, and parents collect their offspring from directly outside the classroom so that there is an opportunity for communication about the child's progress.

Both of these establishments, as well as the other public ones to be described, are attached to primary schools so that the children will usually move up into school from kindergarten with their own age group with a minimum of trauma. It seems likely that these examples are quite representative of public kindergartens in urban areas throughout Japan.

Rural Japan is often divided for sociological purposes into three types based on the economic activities of farming, fishing and lumbering, and it so happened that within easy reach of our base in Tateyama were kindergartens representing populations of the first two of these types. Shirayuri Kindergarten was actually located in a seaside community which had traditionally been based on a fishing economy. The local public kindergarten, named Funakata, provided another institution in the area of our residence, enabling me to make contact with the families of some of the children in their home situations as well. This was a much smaller kindergarten than the more urban ones, with just over a hundred pupils, divided into only three classes. Each of these mixed newcomers with pupils in their second year. The headmaster explained that they had to mix the pupils for practical reasons such as lack of space and staff, but they were able to point out advantages to the parents like the fact that the older children could help to teach the younger ones. Although only about twenty per cent of the children now came from fishing families, the standard of living had been lower in this area than elsewhere and it was one of the duties of such a kindergarten to make up for a possible lack in home training by ensuring that the pupils learned basic matters of hygiene like washing their faces and cleaning their teeth. There was a rather more relaxed atmosphere here than in the larger kindergartens and considerably more so than in Shirayuri.

The same was true of the kindergarten in Miyoshi Village, a farming community close to Tateyama, where the numbers were similar, but the fact that there were four teachers and more classrooms made it possible to have children separated by age into groups of just under thirty pupils. The facilities here were more than ample, due to the recent reconstruction of a new primary school which had previously shared some of the quarters of the kindergarten. Thus there was a playroom for P.E. and band practice as well as a large modern hall, shared by other organisations in the community, for games and dancing. The children came from quite a wide rural catchment area so most of them travelled to and from kindergarten in two private buses. In this respect it resembled Shirayuri, which also ran buses around Tateyama and its environs to collect children from families which had chosen the private establishment, sometimes for this very reason of convenience.

Most children in Tateyama whose mothers are at home during the day attend a kindergarten from their fifth year of life until their seventh, when they enter primary school. Shirayuri accepts pupils two years younger than this so that some parents with conflicting work demands choose it for this reason. However, there are also day nurseries in most parts of the city, which are open from 9 to 5 instead of sending children home after lunch, so mothers working full-time are usually able to find places at an earlier age, and take advantage of the longer hours right up until their children enter school. The usual procedure is to apply for such a place through the City Hall, which runs a kind of clearing house, placing children in the most convenient nursery available, and working out the fees for the parents on the basis of their income and need. Within the city of Tateyama there are six public nurseries, which come directly under the administration of the welfare department, and five private ones, which are approved by and affiliated to the city department.

Again to try and get a representative sample, I visited several of these, spending prolonged periods of time in one public and one private one. Both were situated in quiet back streets with plenty of space outside for play. They were headed by kind, concerned middle-aged ladies who seemed very devoted to their jobs, whereas the public kindergartens often shared a head, usually male, with the primary school to which they were attached. There were not a great number of differences in their modes of operation, largely laid down by the national standards and curriculum. The children were divided into groups which would eventually form school years, and the last two years before school entry were involved in activities very similar to those of the kindergartens. In Tateyama, the maximum number of children in any one nursery was a hundred, but over half of them had only sixty children in total. Of these, the numbers tend to increase for the older groups, and most nurseries do not accept babies until they are weaned on to solid food at about ten months.

Nago, the public nursery, seemed to be fairly representative in this respect, providing separate rooms for six weaned babies, ten infants, sixteen or seventeen each of two- and three-year-olds, and groups of over twenty for the children of kindergarten age, although they were not full up to their maximum quota. The private one, named UNE-SCO nursery and partially funded by the national and prefectural

125

departments of welfare, provided the most comprehensive facilities in the city, taking babies from three months and also providing after-school care for primary school pupils whose parents did not get out of work in time to collect them. However, even here, there were only three babies under a year in age, and again, the classes of kindergarten-age children were the most numerous. The other private day nurseries, including one which was run by a local Christian church, did not accept children under eighteen or nineteen months, one not until they were two years old.

In Kyushu, where I spent the final month of the research period, the situation was rather different. Perhaps because more mothers are working in this area, most of the public funds are channelled into day nurseries, and the only kindergartens available were private ones. Thus the majority of children attend the local day nursery before entering school, while only the better-off, more achievement-oriented parents chose to pay the higher fees the kindergartens charge. It is rather interesting, however, that many adults refer to the establishment attended by their pre-schoolers as a kindergarten (yōchien) even when it is in fact a day nursery (hoikuen). This seems to be quite appropriate because, despite the fact that they are administered at a national level by different ministries, those involved readily admit that there are few major differences between the two types of institution once the children are of kindergarten age.

In this area I visited the two day nurseries attended by children of the village where I had previously conducted research and where I carried out most of the interviews with mothers. Both were set in rural surroundings within walking distance of the community, and catered for some ninety children in similar age proportions to Tateyama. One of them was enclosed within the grounds of a Buddhist temple, situated on a hillside among sweet-smelling pine trees. It was administered by the local priest who proclaimed 'free play' its speciality. The other was located within a populated area, in the grounds of the home of the head teacher, an elderly lady who had been running the nursery since opening it thirty years previously. The equipment seemed older than that of the Tateyama nurseries, and the conditions were somewhat spartan, since the children took their daily rest on the bare wooden floorboards, but in both cases there was the same happy atmosphere found in all such establishments for small children.

The private kindergartens I visited in Kyushu each had their own special characteristics. The two in Yame City, within the administrative boundaries of which the village of Kurotsuchi was situated, were attached to a Buddhist temple and a Christian church, and both made use of Montessori methods. This meant that more time than elsewhere was spent allowing the children to select their own occupations, and a certain amount of time was allocated to religious ritual, but they both exhibited most of the common characteristics of kindergartens more generally. Saishōji, the one attached to a temple, had 155 pupils divided into five classes where three-, four- and five-year-olds were mixed together. Sakae, the Christian one, kept their age groups separate. Most of the children in the latter were not Christian, though they took part in a rote-like fashion in the ceremony, but they attended the kindergarten for its educational reputation. The headmaster explained that most of them came from nuclear families because when grandparents had more influence they usually preferred the more traditional atmosphere of the Buddhist one, which was somewhat ironic since the latter was much more meticulous in using the foreign Montessori learning materials.

During the summer holidays, and therefore in the absence of its pupils, I also visited a very dynamic kindergarten in Kumamoto City, a large urban area with a total of no fewer than forty-eight private kindergartens to supplement the two public ones. Entitled simply Kyushu Music Kindergarten, it trained 260 children in one establishment and 470 in another to take part in concerts and marching displays, even travelling abroad to China on one occasion, as well as developing their individual talents in piano and violin. Like Shirayuri, it also runs after-school classes so that ex-pupils may keep up these accomplishments and study others for which teachers are available. Again, it also seemed to have most of the common characteristics of kindergartens elsewhere.

Finally, I visited the oldest kindergarten in Japan at Ochanomizu Women's University, which was the only one I observed totally to have altered its procedure so that it resembled a European establishment more than it did any of the other kindergartens or day nurseries. Its reputation, both as a well-known and long-established kindergarten and for its attachment to a prestigious university, complete with primary and secondary schools to work through once a place is gained, made it a very popular choice for parents. However, many of them were inevitably disappointed since numbers were limited. Judging by the reading and writing abilities of the children in one of the classes of four-year-olds, they represented a highly achievement-oriented group, borne out by the numbers of them who also attend classes after kindergarten. It was thus interesting that the children in fact spend most of their time playing at whatever happens to take their fancy, which is the latest thing in 'progressive' education. Various other 'different' aspects of this establishment were actually also very Japanese, as will be seen when more has been said about what is usual in Japanese kindergartens.

Common features of pre-school establishments

Despite the variety described in the previous section of the kindergartens and day nurseries visited, there were enough common features to make possible a considerable amount of generalisation about pre-school establishments in Japan. Much of this may well be due to national concern and the legally sanctioned standards, which makes the whole educational system remarkably comprehensive and uniform compared with that found in other nations. I have tried to glean as much as possible of what makes them particularly Japanese, and thus effective as agents of national socialisation. Considering the many common historical elements shared by kindergartens in Japan, the United States and Europe, it is particularly revealing to examine those aspects of such influence which have been selected and developed as appropriate for Japan.

Since the day nurseries are similar in many respects to the kindergartens, the two will be considered together after the chief distinguishing features have been summarised. As a rule, these constitute longer hours for the former and therefore the incorporation into the daily activities of a rest for an hour or two after the midday meal; the provision of nursery nurses to provide the care for the children which they are deemed to lack at home; and a health examination on arrival each day. Babies are looked after in a separate room where home-like conditions are created and their individual feeding and sleeping needs may be met. Here too potties are provided so that they may be trained in their use. Gradually they are introduced to the communal activities of the other children so that, for example, once they can feed themselves, they eat round a table at the times fixed for meals, and begin to participate in the general routine of the establishment. For kindergarten teachers, the training is more stringent than for nursery nurses, and usually involves two to four years at university or junior college.

Lay-out

The usual arrangement, much like Europe and the United States, is for classrooms to be set out around a spacious play area furnished with swings, slides, climbing frames and sand-pits. There are often also areas for simple cultivation of plants and vegetables, and Shirayuri keeps geese, hens and pheasants in pens within the playground. Each classroom is entered through a utility area providing cupboards or shelves for the children's shoes, and pegs on which to hang their coats, hats and bags. It is customary for each child to have personal space marked with a name and symbol so that it can be recognised even before they can read. There are also easily accessible toilets and washing areas where a number of establishments expect children to keep their own towels and possibly toothbrushes too. Once inside the classroom there is another personal space, a shelf or a drawer, in which each child keeps a set of equipment including drawing books, a box containing crayons, felt-tips pens, glue and scissors, plasticine, and, in some cases, castanets and skipping ropes. The details vary from one place to another, but each set is virtually identical for every child within the one establishment, and an important part of the children's training is to learn to take care of their own things and put them away after use.

In England these items are communally used, and this was a way in which Ochanomizu differed from other Japanese kindergartens, although there too the children each had a personal drawer where they kept drawing books, felt-tip pens and scissors. Another important difference in the appearance of English and Japanese kindergartens is in the apparel of the children. In Japan most kindergartens have some kind of uniform, usually identical for boys and girls, although this varies from a complete outfit at Shirayuri and other private establishments to a smock and hat or cap in most of the public ones. Many of them also have a standard bag in which to carry lunch-boxes, handkerchiefs, and notebooks for communication between teachers and parents, as well as providing space for children to take home some of their work. Even the lunch-boxes are fairly similar from one child to another, although these and the bags may be of different colours for girls and boys. In Funakata and other public kindergartens the children were equipped with coloured caps for outside play on hot days and these were of different hues for each class. Ochanomizu had no uniform, no bags and no standard equipment boxes, but each child wore a badge bearing the character for a child of kindergarten age, and an apron to which was pinned a clean handkerchief.

The classrooms are usually gaily decorated with examples of the children's work, often comprising forty almost identical objects, but also sometimes set into a complete collage on various themes, such as fishes in the sea, trees in a wood, people in a train etc. Thus individual efforts are combined into a grand co-operative creation orchestrated by the teacher. Every single establishment visited had a decoration on the wall which listed the individual birthdays of each child in the class. In one case these were written on flowers growing out of pots, each of which represented one month; in another they were chicks breaking out of eggs; frequently those born in the same month were grouped together and it was common practice to hold a celebration for each group, as will be described shortly. Sometimes songs were written up, as were learning aids such as arabic numerals and simple Japanese characters, although most did not teach reading and writing directly. A washing line, hung with drying paper constructions, was commonly seen, too, as was a duty list of children's names and symbols made like a calendar to turn over each day.

Standard furniture includes tables and chairs to accommodate each child, although these are sometimes stored away when not in use to increase the amount of floor space available; a piano or organ in each classroom; television, record player; and a blackboard on which is written at least the day and date and sometimes the number of children present. In some places the floor is marked out with coloured tape to help the children stand in rows, or sit in a circle, but at Shirayuri this was removed for the classroom used by the oldest group. Usually there is a magazine stand with various books and pamphlets for the children to use, and a bookcase with story books for the teacher.

The number of toys available varies a great deal from place to place, although all provide the building blocks prescribed by the national standards. Otherwise there is sometimes a corner with *tatami* matting and miniature equipment for children to play house, and the Montessori kindergartens provide a variety of educational toys such as jigsaws, sewing pictures and construction sets. Shirayuri had no toys other than the blocks, except in the class for the smallest children, the head teacher explaining that she preferred the children to play imaginatively with natural materials. Ochanomizu had the greatest variety of toys, which was probably the way in which it most resembled English kindergartens and play groups. Here, too, the children seemed more capable than those in even the Montessori kindergartens of choosing something of their own to do and getting on with it without help from a teacher. The chief difference, then, between this and most Japanese kindergartens is that the infants are given a greater chance to make their own decisions in the course of their time there, but this is something which will be more forcibly illustrated in subsequent sections.

Finally, classrooms are usually abundantly supplied with living things such as flowers, goldfish, tortoises and a variety of seasonably available insects and crustacea. In the summer, for example, children collect and bring in innumerable crayfish, which can be caught in irrigation ditches, as well as the huge beetles and cicadas which can be found virtually wherever there are trees. Many children keep such prizes in little boxes and cages, so that the teacher encourages a classroom collection in order to teach their owners how to feed them and clean them out from time to time. Other natural objects such as pine cones, shells and so forth probably bear witness to class outings of the past few weeks.

General activities

It is not intended here to describe each of the 137 activities recommended by the Ministry of Education for kindergartens but to give an idea of how the six main categories into which they are divided are covered, and to formulate some generalisations about how the activities in Japanese kindergartens and day nurseries are peculiarly Japanese. To describe the activities themselves would certainly not achieve the second of these aims. Here, as elsewhere, children spend time drawing pictures, making paper constructions with glue and scissors, singing lustily in unison, playing musical instruments, doing exercises in time to music, planting seeds in pots or attending to their growing plants and vegetables. The time spent on *origami* may be greater here than elsewhere, but that is a detail. They also spend considerable time listening to their teacher reading stories, or passing pictures through a 'paper theatre', and there is plenty of chance for less formal conversation between the teacher and her pupils. The content of the stories, plays and conversations provides fertile ground for an investigation of the values being passed on, and the categories covered here include road safety, legends and myths, folklore and morals.

To give an example of this, a popular children's story in Japan is the one entitled 'The peach boy' (*Momotarō*). It is an ancient folk tale with a familiar theme about an old childless couple who find a large peach, out of which emerges a boy for them to bring up. As in stories elsewhere, when the boy reaches an appropriate age, he sets off on a brave mission to overcome an evil force, in this case an island of demons, which threatens the well-being of ordinary citizens of the land. He is of course successful, and praised for his bravery, but the particularly Japanese aspect of this story is how he collects on his way to the island a variety of helpers – different in different versions – but always at first quarrelling amongst themselves and eventually persuaded by Momotarō to co-operate in their common venture.

The same theme of co-operation has been neatly introduced into the originally English story of the 'Three little pigs'. In a popular version in England the first two little pigs, who built their houses of straw and wood, are eaten up by the wolf, who is finally outwitted by the clever third little pig who not only builds his house of bricks, which thus withstands the huffing and puffing of the wolf, but also entices single-handed his predator down the chimney to his death in the cooking pot. The same end meets the wolf in the Japanese version, but not until the first two little pigs have escaped from their flimsy homes to join and co-operate with the third little pig in his effort to catch the wolf. The three then live happily ever after. Even this modification did not satisfy some four year-olds who were watching a hand-puppet play of the story at their day nursery. As soon as the mother pig sent her charges off down the road to fend for themselves, a couple of smart boys at the back began calling 'why don't you build a house together? It's much better to co-operate, you know!'

It is a noticeable feature in many Japanese kindergartens that activities are often carried out almost simultaneously by everyone in the class. Thus, for example, there will be a time for colouring, when each child will be issued with a piece of paper with identical shapes on them. Together they will colour the square red, the triangle yellow and the circle green. Another time they will all follow the teacher's demonstrations and make paper crabs, together cutting out the parts, colouring in the appropriate places, applying the glue, and fitting the pieces into place. *Origami* is particularly suited to this approach and the teacher goes round the class helping small children after she has demonstrated a step in the procedure. Singing in unison also plays an important part in these establishments, and most children memorise a large number of songs, varying with the seasons and special occasions which arise.

Teachers emphasise that the large numbers in their classrooms make such an approach necessary, and the situation is not so different from the French *maternelles*.[4] However, this aspect of kindergarten life is less common in the Montessori schools and other private establishments like Ochanomizu which boast the 'progressive' approach. Here, like England and the United States many of the resources are available all day so that children may choose different activities depending on their mood and inclinations. To capture the real essence of the Japanese kindergarten or day nursery, I think one needs to look rather at the overall structure of the day, and indeed year, and the way in which habits are inculcated in small children.

The headmaster of Funakata kindergarten said that basically this was his concern, to teach habits for living, and an examination of, first, the daily structure and, secondly, that for the year will reveal many principles of training familiar from previous chapters of this book.

Structure of the day

On arrival in the morning, children must go through the usual entry/exit ritual of taking off their outdoor shoes, changing into indoor ones, and storing away their outdoor ones in their places. They hang up their coats, hats and bags, and if appropriate change into their indoor smocks and aprons. They may then be expected to stamp a page for attendance in their notebook and leave it for the teacher to communicate, if necessary, with parents. It is of course necessary to do much of this at any kindergarten, but it is the ritual element which is notable here. Children are actually shown the proper way to do all these things as, or even before, they start kindergarten, and the teacher may help them if they have trouble at first. The little ones need assistance, of course, and much of the first term is concerned with learning routines such as these, but even three-year-olds are usually helping one another after a few weeks, and by four, the movements become almost automatic. It helps that the shoe routine is also essential at home, so that even the tiniest children are aware that their shoes must be removed on entry. At Shirayuri the outdoor uniforms have buttons down the back, so most children must ask a friend to help change these, and the teacher sometimes arranges them all in a circle, each one attending to the child in front.

At Shirayuri, the day begins proper when the teacher sits down to play a lullaby melody on the piano. It is the same tune each day and it is the signal for the children to sit down in a circle. They should clasp their knees and remain quiet until all are seated. The teacher keeps playing the same tune over and over again until everyone complies and those first seated cast angry looks at the laggers to make sure that they hurry up. Once they are ready, she breaks into a contrasting drill which is the new signal for everyone to jump to their feet. It is followed by a cadence to which they all bow nicely, after which she plays the introduction to the good morning song. Again all this is practised during the early days until it becomes an automatic response. It is the same song each morning so everyone joins in with great gusto. At the end of the song the teacher says 'good morning', at Shirayuri in English, and the children chorus their reply. There may be an inspection of uniform at this stage, and a few will be straightened up or have their shoes changed to the appropriate feet, after which the teacher reads the register. Each child answers clearly to his or her name and sits down. In the top class, the children are expected to keep count of the number of absentees so that they can announce this in English to the teacher at the end.

Other establishments have variant forms of this ritual in the mornings, usually making use of the piano or organ rather than the teacher's voice to instil order, which seems to be one explanation why such an instrument is a prescribed part of the equipment. It is also a compulsory part of a kindergarten teacher's training to be able to play. In several places there is also a period of exercise first thing when the children carry out various fixed movements in time to piano, organ or records, amplified for relay into the playground during dry weather. It is often the case that the children have a period of free play before this, while everyone is arriving, and it thus provides a ritual beginning to the day's communal activities. At Saishōji, in Yame, where the Montessori equipment is freely available for use for a rather long period, the priest who directs the kindergarten was at the gate to greet each child personally on the day when I visited.

Various activities will follow this fixed ritual in the mornings, but the same principles come into play again at break time, when milk may be distributed, and also before lunch. If things are spread about the classroom after the previous activity, the teacher will call out, or play another fixed tune, to indicate that it is clearing-up time. At Kyushu Music Kindergarten, there is a special 'clearing away' song at such times. Each child must put away personal belongings in the appropriate place and everyone helps clear the tables, or bring them out, to prepare for the next event. If it involves eating, hands must be washed, toilets visited – at one kindergarten there was a tune for this too – tables may need to be wiped, and children on duty for that day distribute the milk and other items needed for the repast. If packed lunch has been brought, this must be laid ready on a napkin. All is carried out in an orderly fashion which is taught in the early days, and once the children are used to it, the teacher may again use the piano or organ to play a special lunch or break tune until the preparations are made. There may then be a pre-lunch or pre-break song – in one day nursery to the tune known in England as 'Chopsticks' – and often there is a ritual exchange of phrases between the children on duty and those sitting ready to eat.

For example, at Miyoshi Kindergarten, the children on duty stood at the front when they had finished giving out the milk and the others sat with their hands on their heads when they had laid out their lunch. Those at the front chorused a polite phrase meaning approximately 'are all the preparations made?' and the others replied 'they are made'; 'then let us sing the lunch song' came from the front. Following the song, they all joined in the usual pre-eating phrase of thanks and it was at last time to eat. In Tateyama Kindergarten the routine was only slightly different. The children on duty waited at the front until all the others had returned from washing their hands to call out 'has everyone returned to their seats?' 'Yes' they replied; 'has everyone got their hands on their knees?' Again 'yes'; 'then we will give out the milk'. Once the distribution was complete, they asked 'has everyone received milk?' 'Yes'; 'has everyone a straw?' 'Yes'; 'then let us receive it'. The words are formulated into fixed phrases and the children on duty pronounce them simultaneously in a ritual fashion.

No one begins eating before the ritual has been enacted, and children who misbehave are reprimanded by their friends if not by those on duty at the front. The more time it takes to complete the preparations, the hungrier they get, so it is to the advantage of all that things run smoothly, which makes for very effective peer group discipline.

The end of the meal or snack is also marked ritually by the use of a stylised phrase of appreciation, after which the children go through a routine of repacking their lunch boxes, stacking their cups, throwing away their rubbish and washing their hands. Again, things must be done properly, although this time they need not wait for all to be ready since those who finish early are able to look at magazines or go out to play depending on the day's plan.

A smaller ritual may mark off time allocated to particular activities. For example, story time is found in all establishments, and once the children are sitting ready the teacher may announce 'the beginning', or 'the story', after which the children may be expected to clap. At the end too the teacher will pronounce in a stylised fashion 'that's the end' and again there will be clapping. The phrases used here may be compared to the words which will be familiar to anyone growing up in England with post-war radio for children: 'Are you sitting comfortably? Then I'll begin.' They are repeated constantly, unchanged, and they mark out a predictable time and event. Music practice, too, is often distinguished in this way in Japanese establishments. The children may have to stand to attention, or sit up straight, even chorus a request for the teacher to begin, and at the end they will join together in a bow as they pronounce a stylised phrase of thanks to the instructor. This rite is repeated even in private music lessons.

An element of prescription and order is even introduced into what may be described as 'free expression', such as children's reports on their own activities outside the kindergarten. There may be time each morning for children to bring 'news' to the class, and here children are encouraged to order their information under the categories 'who?', 'when?', 'where?', 'what?' and 'how?', so that the speech in which they make such statements becomes gradually more stylised as they get older and more articulate. This training is good preparation for primary school, when speaking in front of the class is generally in rather formalised language.

At the day nurseries there is also some ritual attached to preparations for rest time. In some cases the children change into their pyjamas, and mattresses and pillows are laid out in tidy rows. When everyone is tucked in ready the caretaker may read them a story or sing softly until they fall asleep. For very small children there may be two or three caretakers sitting amongst the mattresses rubbing their backs. Sometimes older children are allowed to look at books or magazines for a while. Once the rest time is over each child will store away its bedding in a cupboard and change again into daytime clothes. By establishing routine activities of this sort, and encouraging each child to take care of its own property, the caretakers minimise their own work as well as training the children in the daily habits which are emphasised again and again as important aspects of pre-school education.

Finally, each day there is a ritual to be performed before the class breaks up and the children return to their own individual homes. This usually allows about half an hour for preparations such as changing into outdoor clothes, retrieving the communication booklet from the teacher and packing away any other notes or work to be taken home. In some cases the children on duty will formally pass on their charge to the next incumbents, and all will pronounce phrases of thanks to the ones who have carried out their tasks, and of request to those who will follow the next day. The children may then stand to attention and bow to the teacher and to each other as they pronounce phrases of farewell, they may sing a final song, or they may join in a final prayer at establishments with a religious foundation. At Sakae Christian kindergarten in Yame, for example, the routine involved piano music to indicate that the children should sit ready with their hats and bags on; a change of rhythm for a final routine of hand movements and song; a change of tune while children put heads on hands, yawn and look sleepy; a break while papers to take home are distributed; another tune when arms are crossed over chests; a musical prayer with hands together; a chord to bring the children to attention on their feet; the stacking of tables and chairs; and a final ditty for a good-bye song involving clapping, marching and waving to each other; after which each child individually shakes the teacher's hand. As the youngsters finally left the classroom a loudspeaker brought a record of 'going-home' music out into the playground and surrounding neighbourhood. The details vary somewhat from one place to another, but there is invariably some form of ritual to mark the end of the communal day and separate this from the family lives to which the children will then return.

It should perhaps be pointed out here that the emphasis on order in specific parts of the kindergarten day does not in any way subdue the spirit and liveliness of the youngsters involved. Rather to the contrary, perhaps, for the children are aware of clear distinctions between times when they may shout and play, which they do with as much enthusiasm as children anywhere, and times when they are expected, almost automatically, to sit quietly and achieve a degree of control over their exhuberance. Thus while the ritual has obvious advantages in the management of large numbers of small children, it also serves to train each individual member of the group to establish orderly personal habits and control his or her bodily activities.

Structure of the year

Pre-school education in Japan also pays considerable attention to making children aware of the cyclical nature of the passage of time on a larger scale, and this combines traditional events and divisions with the modern calendar introduced only just over a century ago. The week is distinguished, as it is now in many industrialised countries, by the provision of a day off on Sundays. Most kindergartens also have half-days on Wednesdays and Saturdays, and day nurseries just on Saturdays. Regular weekly events may be organised to help children learn their days of the week, which also appear in songs and other mnemonic devices. The months are differentiated in almost all these establishments, it seems, by dividing the children into groups according to the month in which they were born. Their names are displayed on the classroom wall in clusters for each of the months, as already described, and the appropriate groups are honoured each month with a collective birthday party.

This is quite an event, attended by all the classes together, who learn and perform songs for each other. The children who have celebrated their birthdays that month are seated, perhaps wearing special hats or crowns, at the front, where they are expected to stand up in turn and announce clearly to the assembly the number of years they have attained. This is done in a stylised manner again, each child announcing, for example, 'I am Hanako of Yurigumi and I have become five years old'. A birthday song may well be sung, perhaps repeated enough times to include the names of all the children concerned. The event usually also includes some kind of entertainment provided by the teachers. On one occasion I witnessed they did a puppet show of the story of the Three Little Pigs, on another one of the teachers came in adorned with a large, furry dog's head and talked to the children. At Ochanomizu Kindergarten the mothers of the children who have had birthdays are invited to participate. The event may be concluded with the serving of a treat to each child in place of their usual mid-morning snack. The gathering of the whole assembly of children on these occasions also provides an opportunity for the teachers to encourage the older ones to display their skills as 'big brothers' and 'big sisters', and to set an example to the younger children in their behaviour and their singing, for example. The songs are performed by each class in turn, preceded and concluded by a formal bow, and appreciated with clapping afterwards.

Other events which involve the assembly of the whole establishment are also often concerned with the marking of the passage of time. The year is divided into three school terms, and each term is marked at the beginning and the end with an opening and closing ceremony. At the beginning of the scholastic year, in April, there is a special event to introduce new pupils into the establishment, and, at Shirayuri, the parents of the new pupils are also invited. This is a veritable celebration of an important step in life and the children concerned are often given gifts by relatives at this time. The kindergarten handed out posies to each mother as she arrived, and the new children were presented with their class badges. Once assembled in the hall, the older children sang the kindergarten song, and the headmistress was introduced as a 'replacement mummy'. Each new child had its name read out, to which the response '*hai*' was expected, and everyone clapped, the more loudly the clearer the response. Each of the teachers then introduced themselves and said a few words, after which the founder and the head of the PTA made speeches. The occasion closed with further singing, and the new children were then photographed with their new mothers and their new teachers, to provide a glossy momento of the event.

At the establishments with religious foundation there was of course some appropriate ritual during these gatherings, but the secular assemblies were also highly formalised. The talks given to the children seem to emphasise the opportunities for them to be surrounded by friends and companions, and they are exhorted to play harmoniously with one another. At the Buddhist Montessori kindergarten in Yame the children chanted a phrase about how they were going to try and carry out this ideal: 'let us play happily and healthily together' is an approximate translation of the slogan. At the end of term at Shirayuri, the headmistress gave a talk about appropriate behaviour for the holidays, and the children who had attended every single day of the term were presented with rewards.

Apart from these artificially created divisions of time, the natural passage of the seasons is also remembered in various ways in pre-school curricula. Japan's climate is even more clearly divided than that of northern Europe into spring, summer, autumn and winter, marked by changes in the weather and in the life cycle of plants and trees. These changes are reinforced culturally by the use of different clothes, different street decorations and different activities deemed appropriate to each of the seasons. These change on specific days of the year, which may be marked by the preparation and consumption of special foods.

At kindergartens and day nurseries, songs and stories are often chosen to correspond to the current season, and the Shirayuri song book comes in four volumes, one for each of the seasons of the year. Thus as children move into their second and third years there, they recognise the songs they learnt the previous year recurring with the season. Activities classed under the general heading of 'nature study' inevitably reflect this division of time, but it tends to pervade all areas. Music and language have already been mentioned, in the use of seasonally varying songs and stories; health is concerned with dressing appropriately and being aware of the dangers of the extremes of temperatures and their sudden changes; the study of society includes local responses to seasonal variations in farming, fishing, sericulture etc., as well as the more independent elements of an industrial society; and the creations of drawing and handiwork regularly reflect the objects and activities of the current season.

As well as days concerned with the changing seasons, the Japanese calendar also has an abundance of other special days denoting modern and ancient festivals, remembering important historic events, and honouring particular categories of people. Most of these are observed in pre-school establishments where the teacher talks to the children about the significance of the day in question, reads them stories and teaches them songs, where relevant, and helps them to make gifts for their relatives in the appropriate categories. Thus, once a year, mothers, fathers and grandparents are presented with examples of their children's handiwork on their own particular day, and children are exhorted to appreciate and remember the work that each of these relatives does for and with them, singing about their qualities during several days around that time. Aspects of Japanese history and mythology are learned through such annual observances, as are popular superstitions about the existence of demons. Japan is not unusual in making use of annual events to supply themes and ideas for the activities of small children, but here they are classed as 'social studies' and many important values of Japanese society are being passed on. There is often also a good measure of moral content such as being kind and thinking of others.

Annually, too, there may be events which require weeks of preparation, such as sports day and recitals. The former was held during our stay at Shirayuri and ably illustrated some of the ways in which more general values are incorporated into such occasions. Typically, in the West, sports day is an occasion for the recognition of individual achievement and competitive spirit. Races for which the winner receives a prize form the basis of the proceedings and any other activities are but icing on the cake of competition. Not so the Japanese version. Races are held, to be sure, but they almost all involve some kind of co-operation as an integral part of the event, and individuals represent a larger group such as their class or residential district. All the children wear reversible red or white caps, and most of the races are between reds and whites. At the end of the day every single child receives a prize and possibly a medal is hung about their necks.

Parents are expected to attend and, in the case of Shirayuri, it was a real show to demonstrate the achievements of the kindergarten as a whole. The teachers were immaculately turned out in white, and the children wore identical sports clothes which had been ordered for the occasion. The first event was a drumming display by the children of the oldest class, who had been rehearsing daily for weeks. They later put on a cheer-leading-type routine which they had also been hard at work perfecting. Each of the other classes had a chance to sing and dance also, one of the songs being the previously quoted ditty extolling the virtues of their daddies. Individual achievement was not neglected, but it was channelled into the glory of the whole group. Thus the relay race gave the fast runners a chance to excel, but they had been chosen earlier to represent their classes, and the sticks were passed between members of different classes who lived in the same zones of the city. Thus the spectators could spur on the participants on both counts. Other races involved parents and children co-operating in carrying an enormous soft ball, or tied together three-legged style, and the most popular event of the whole day seemed to be the tug of war when the entire red team took on the entire white one. The line of parents with cameras at the side attested to the value placed on this supreme example of co-operative skill. It seemed appropriate, if somewhat shameful at the time, that the only child to refuse to participate was my own English son.

The only races with outright winners were those held between parents, and as they involved obstacles and a version of musical chairs, they were probably more accurately classed as games. Nevertheless, the latter was accorded an Olympic-style presentation of gold, silver and bronze paper crowns, perched in place by the children of the champions, in this case involving the pushy Western author in second place! The order of the day had been effort, enjoyment and a chance for the children to show off and have fun with their parents, especially fathers, whose enthusiasm the head teacher no doubt valued as assurance of the following year's income.

Thus the annual cycle is established and repeated in predictable events which fit in for the most part with national expectations. Ceremonies and festivals, some of which were described in Chapter I, are nowadays nationally standardised, with only minor regional variation. The same occasions are remembered at home, at kindergarten, and reports about them appear on television. As well as learning daily habits, and the art of group interaction, then, the children are also being nationalised; they are beginning to be Japanese citizens.

Peer group pressure

Apart from the form and content of pre-school education, the chief difference for a child from its previous home life is the existence of a large number of other children with whom it must share the facilities. At home it has had the benefit of a good deal of individual attention from adults who are emotionally committed to its care, and even if it belongs to a large group of siblings, which is becoming increasingly unusual these days, it has a definite place in the hierarchy, and specific roles to play. At kindergarten or nursery, it is just one of a large number of equally important children of the same or similar ages, under the guidance of an adult who will usually remain with the group no longer than one school year. At first, this may seem quite overwhelming, but many of the children will move together through the whole of the school system, and the socialising influence of this peer group seems to be particularly strong. The teachers and other adults direct activities, but they also cultivate and frequently take advantage of peer group pressure.

The first lesson that a child must learn is that the fun and friendship of kindergarten (or nursery) are for those who co-operate, who become active and enthusiastic members of the inside group. Much of the time this involves doing exactly what everyone else is doing, and occasionally one sees an individual dissident refusing to join in. Such a child may be left outside the classroom, or standing apart from the rest of the children in the playground. For the most part it is ignored. The teacher is involved with making life enjoyable for perhaps thirty-nine other children and there is little time left for the difficult one. One case I observed involved quite a small boy who kept wetting his pants. The teacher would come out from time to time to change him and encourage him to come in, but she made little fuss. If he refused, she just left him again. He came into the classroom at lunch time but didn't eat every much. Again the teacher said a few words of encouragement, but he was largely ignored, by the children as well. Indeed, the teacher encouraged the children to ostracise him by pointing him out as 'strange' and 'peculiar' (*okashii*), words applied to any child who cries or looks unhappy at kindergarten. 'Fancy not wanting to come to kindergarten', she had said at the beginning, 'what a funny boy.' And to the boy, she had said 'come and join in, don't be a baby'. In a similar situation at another kindergarten, a girl who had been refusing to dance was praised when she eventually began to join in, with the words 'now you've become a big sister'.

Indeed, so unpleasant must it be for such dissidents that as time goes by there are very few to be seen. All the children learn that the fun is on the inside, joining in, and I only saw about three such cases during the whole of the research period, which included the early part of the school year. The case of Totto-chan, the self-portrayed protagonist of the best-selling novel by Tetsuko Kuroyanagi, is perhaps the exception that proves the rule. As a girl the author was expelled from her first primary school because the teachers could not cope with her extraordinary behaviour. She did indeed spend much time outside the classroom, or at the window, as the subtitle of the book indicates, in Japanese using a phrase – *madogiwa no* – which, as the author explains in the English version, also means 'out in the cold' or 'left out'. Fortunately for Totto-chan, her mother found her another school which could cope with her idiosyncrasies, and this is what the book is largely about.[5]

The same sort of treatment is meted out to children who cry at kindergarten, even if they are hurt. Their wounds will be treated, but no one cuddles them better, as they might in the West; at most they are given a hand to hold, often that of another child. They are exhorted not to cry, that to cry is *okashii*, 'strange', and 'peculiar' and it is often pointed out that no one else is crying, they are crying alone. Other children may even point at them and laugh, but eventually they are just ignored. In contrast, a child who falls over and gets bravely up again is praised for being strong. Children should be happy and cheerful; to cry is to be different, and to be the same as everyone else is an ideal greatly encouraged at kindergarten. Mothers start this kind of training before their children enter kindergarten, but the force of ostracism is made much clearer when there are so many examples of cheerfulness to contend with. At one nursery I noticed that children who had been hit by another whimpered quietly for a while and eventually controlled their crying. Thus they were achieving self-discipline through experience in a group. At this stage it may be indirect use of group pressure, but the other children are quick to comply and laugh at or ignore the 'strange' child who has yet to achieve self-control.

Making use of similar principles, the teacher may make an example of a child who misbehaves by isolating it from the rest of the class in some way and then calling on the class to express disapproval. Thus, for example, if one or two children talk during the time that the register is being read, she may miss out their names so that they remain standing at the end when all the others are seated. She may then ask the other children whether it is all right to talk during register. The children seem to take a pride in putting their friends right in such cases and chorus 'no' in answer to the teacher's question. The teacher continues for a minute or two to make the recalcitrants feel uncomfortable before allowing them to sit down.

A child may also be brought out to the front to suffer such scorn, and this method of discipline was used very effectively during exercises at Shirayuri. The two older classes, usually divided into separate rooms, were brought together into the big hall for certain events, on one occasion to do exercises to the music of a record. From time to time a child who was showing something less than the one-hundred per cent concentration and enthusiasm which seemed to be expected would be brought up on to the stage to carry out the routine entirely alone. The teacher would ask 'Is it all right to look out of the window?' It is no doubt especially mortifying to be shown up in this way in front of the other class as well as one's inside group. In a similar situation during drum practice for the sports day a child whose eyes wandered away from the conductor at the front, perhaps to glance outside at the sunshine, was almost reduced to tears when the teacher suggested that he go out and join the younger children playing on the grass. He begged to be allowed to stay, and when this was eventually granted became a model participant for the rest of the period. The double humiliation of being separated from the group and relegated to play with the babies was evidently a very strong sanction. These examples seem harsh, and indeed Shirayuri did enforce discipline quite strictly by the final year of kindergarten, but the children who participated properly in all the activities seemed greatly to enjoy themselves as they put their very hearts and souls into everything they did.

It has already been noted in passing that the teacher's use of the piano or organ to indicate to the children that they should sit down, or make preparations for lunch time, was quite effective in putting the onus for discipline on the children themselves, rather than imposing it from above. Those who are slow to comply keep the others waiting and are subject to reprimand from their own peers. The same principle applies to any children whose individual activities hold up the proceedings of the group. This would seem to be close to what Piaget describes as 'the true discipline that the children themselves have willed and consented to'.[6] In *The Moral Judgement of the Child* he points out that a child is not limited in his behaviour to rules laid down by parents and teachers but also ties himself down to all sorts of rules in every sphere of his activity, and especially in that of play. These two types of rules represent two types of authority: in the first case, that of constraint, which he sees as bound up with unilateral respect, and in the latter case, that of mutual agreement and co-operation. The former, he argues, remains external to the child's spirit and does not lead to as effective an obedience as the adult would wish; the latter, on the contrary, takes root inside the child's mind and 'results in an effective observance in the measure in which they are incorporated in an autonomous will'.[7] Thus these Japanese teachers, wittingly or unwittingly, would seem to be making effective use of Piaget's suggestion that educationalists try to harness the efforts children make to impose rules on themselves.[8]

Teachers may also actively seek the judgement of other children in case of fights or disputes amongst them. Typically, in case of a quarrel, the adult will ask others standing nearby who started it and what they think should be done about it. The ideal of playing harmoniously is a strong one and the resolution of a dispute usually involves one or both participants apologising to the other, who must accept the apology, after which both may make use of the Western custom of shaking hands. Teachers commented to me that there are very few quarrels once the children get to know each other, and when there are they are usually resolved by the children themselves. They also noted that the criticism of other children holds much more weight than that of the teacher, whose direct words they may or may not heed, whereas those of other children they usually do. Similar findings have been reported by other observers of peer groups in Japan,[9] and this seems to form a foundation for the general principles of self-control in the interests of an inside group.

The duty system found in all pre-school establishments visited, including Ochanomizu, formalises this form of internal discipline in a very egalitarian way. The various tasks to be performed, which include both serving and directing the others, are carried out by small groups of children in turn. In Tateyama kindergarten the teacher had ordered her pupils by height in one classroom and then written down their names in this order. She then divided the total number into groups of four, wrote their names on separate cards, and these were turned over each day giving a new group the charge. Apart from the serving of milk and meals, which has already been described, the children on duty may have various other tasks to perform. At Saishōji, the Buddhist kindergarten in Yame, there was an opening ceremony which involved the lighting of candles and the present-ation of flowers to a Buddhist altar by these children. In Miyoshi, the children on duty were responsible for lining up their companions ready to march to the hall, a charge they accomplished by standing in front of the rows and calling commands, army style. Thus the duties may involve service, privilege and command, each distributed equally amongst the group, which seems effectively to ensure a maximum of co-operation since no one is likely to undermine a position they will themselves have shortly to hold.

Another positive use of peer group pressure is an appeal to have respect for the collectivity, personalised in the term *mina-san*. *Mina* may be translated as 'everyone' or 'all', and *san* is the term of respect added to a person's name. At Miyoshi kindergarten, for example, one of the teachers constantly addressed her class as *mina-san*, to which the whole class would reply *hai*. The exchange was made in a harmonious sort of singing tone which the children obviously enjoyed, and she would continue with words such as 'are you ready?', 'are you trying hard?' 'are you looking?', each of which would elicit a chorus of positive response, and divert any individuals from private interests and activities. Sometimes children would be reprimanded in an indirect way as a teacher reported some mis-demeanor she had observed, without giving names, and ask *mina-san* whether this was good behaviour. As they chorused 'no', a few faces might look ashamed. Again, as a new activity was described to the children, the teacher would ask *mina-san* if they thought they'd be able to do it. After a chorus of positive response, she would ask if there was anyone who thought they could not. A few might reply, but their tones were uncertain, the more so the fewer there were of them.

The concept of collective ownership is important in the training given to children to look after the property of the establishment to which they belong. 'These things belong to *mina-san*', says the teacher, 'so we must all take good care of them.' This attitude is ritualised at Shirayuri when children sit ready to go home on the buses. Before the engine is started, the children must recite in unison:

Basu no naka de shizuka ni shimashō.	Let's be quiet in the bus.
Mina no basu desukara taisetsu ni shimashō.	It's everyone's bus so we must take care of it.
Basu no naka wa kirei ni shimashō.	Let's keep the inside of it clean.

In their capacity as collective owners of the vehicle, they then make a formal request each day for the driver to take them home.

Principles of institutional training

I think it has been illustrated that most of the aims and aspirations outlined in Chapter III are reinforced in the institutional environment. Much time is still spent inculcating basic habits and continuing the *shitsuke* of parents. A new set of ritual phrases defines a larger inside group of classmates, and distinguishes between the various events and activities of the day and year. Personal identity is maintained in the care of individual sets of equipment and the encouragement of abilities systematically to look after one's own needs. Qualities of endurance and effort are appreciated, as are those of thoughtfulness and compliance, which are now channelled into the wider ideals of harmony and co-operation with the group. There is little indulgence of shortcomings such as selfishness and a propensity for self-pity since individuals become aware of the equally important needs of other individuals, on the one hand, and the new collective entity to which they belong on the other. Hierarchical phrases based on age are also reinforced as older children are encouraged to help and set an example to younger ones. Children who behave or improve are praised as big brothers or big sisters, and when they misbehave, or cry, they are dubbed 'baby' and exhorted to be a big brother or sister. The teacher is an appropriate figure to whom respect may be shown in the use of polite language quite different from that accorded friends and family.

The techniques of training are also comparable to those found in the home and neighbourhood, described in Chapter IV. Again, great emphasis is placed on creating a pleasant *atmosphere* where children can learn through the fun of playing harmoniously with a classful of friends. The premises are gay and colourful, there is an abundance of cheerful music, and the teachers speak in kind, encouraging tones. They also make great efforts to set an *example* to their charges, pronouncing loudly the ritual phrases they expect from the children, and carrying out their activities with them, clearly demonstrating all the required movements. When children are to wash their hands the teacher will wash hers, when they are to clean their teeth the teacher will clean hers. If the children's singing is too raucous, or too timid, the teacher will demonstrate the difference between their present singing and that she feels would be better, appealing to the children to choose which they'd prefer to hear. As already described, older children are often encouraged to set a good example to the younger ones, and in Funakata Kindergarten, where the age groups are mixed, many daily activities follow the pattern of demonstration by older children.

Repetition is again used abundantly in pre-school establishments where so much ritual is brought into play and children are almost conditioned to respond to chords and tunes on the piano and organ. Exercises and songs are repeated time and time again, but the real force of this method lies in the routines associated with so many activities, and the little phrases which are used almost automatically as time goes by. There is less opportunity for the patient *solicitude* shown by mothers, but teachers are certainly not averse to putting forward *explanations* for why children should participate in various activities, especially when they might at first seem reluctant, or when they misbehave. One teacher described the method she uses with children who are unwilling to co-operate in the youngest class at Shirayuri where she explains to them the reason for doing things and then waits, ignoring them if they refuse at first to join in. Eventually they join in.

The positive and negative sanctions used may also be compared to those described in Chapter IV. Again praise is accorded children who try especially hard or do something particularly well. At Shirayuri the headmistress and her secretary would often pop their heads into a classroom as they went by and comment on the singing, or pick out a child to praise, or perhaps to chastise, thus reinforcing the idea that an outsider is a suitable person to comment on the achievements of members of an inside group, in this representing the class as a whole. Rewards are used rarely – even the sports day only provides opportunities for children to help their particular group excel – and the only case observed was that mentioned of children who have managed through the luck of good health to attend every day of term. The reward of the teacher's benevolence is for those who contribute to the smooth and harmonious running of activities, which may be compared to the use of sweets and other treats for children who co-operate in the smooth running of a household.

With regard to punishment, the smack is used in some pre-school establishments, but again this is administered in a rather ritual fashion with an explanation to the recalcitrant and surrounding observers of the reason why, and it seems designed to hurt the child's pride more than anything else. Evidently the most effective negative sanction is again the isolation of the child from the group and the withdrawal of the usual benevolence the teacher metes out to her charges. This may involve physical removal of a child from the room, or separation in other ways, but the strongest aspect of the sanction is the way ridicule is employed involving all the other members of the group. Again, the threat of such ostracism is usually enough for older children, especially if it suggests they may be excluded from some special event, but I did hear younger children being warned that a wicked spirit would come and eat their ears, so the supernatural element may be used here too.

At Shirayuri there was a specific activity designed to develop courage, but it was reserved for the boys. The land owned by the kindergarten included a small hill, with a steep, winding path leading to the summit. Normally it was forbidden territory to the children who were frightened away from it with tales of snakes and the possibility of falling. In their final year, however, boys are taken up quite dangerous routes 'to develop their strength and courage', while girls stay behind and tend the plants below. It is an excursion into the dangerous world normally outside the safety of the kindergarten compound, but successfully accomplished by those who obey instructions and cooperate with their inside group. It is also one of the few occasions when activities are decided on the basis of gender.

Again, the use of specific positive and negative sanctions is limited and several teachers emphasised the importance of maintaining goodwill and happiness in the institutional environment. Hence the emphasis on fun and friendship, harmony and cooperation. Cheerful tunes are used for discipline rather than an angry voice. Quarrels are resolved in a conciliatory way amongst the children themselves. Moral training is carried out through the enjoyment of stories and the celebration of special events. The collective unit is ritually defined and belonging to it is made so attractive that being left out is sufficient punishment to ensure considerable self-control and personal training at the individual level.

Thus it may be seen that pre-school establishments operate largely on the same principles, and with the same ends in view, as do parents and other caretakers of individual children. The public element in child-rearing no doubt contributes to this congruence of approach, but it seems also to reflect certain basic collective ideas about children in general. The chief aim is to bring up children to be Japanese, and the introduction to institutional life, which has been described in this chapter, is an important part of the training.

Notes

1 These national standards, and those which follow, are laid out in English in *Pre-School Education in Japan* 1981: 2–7.
2 *Ibid.* 10–11, 3–4.
3 *Ibid.* 9.
4 Deasey 1978: 202–14.
5 Kuroyanagi 1981 (Japanese) and 1982 (English): 198.
6 Piaget 1932: 367.
7 *Ibid.* 365; this is not unlike the point made by Raum (1940: 388) in reference to Chaga children.
8 *Ibid.* 364–5.
9 Singer 1973: 34; Maretzki & Maretzki 1963: 129, 169–70.

Chapter Six

The world view presented to the child

Having examined from the adult point of view the agents, their aims, and the methods they use in the training of small children, I propose now to try to build up a picture of the world view being presented. This is not a report of interviews with children but an analysis of the treatment they receive, which attempts to identify some salient features of the system of classification underlying the approach. Certain basic principles have emerged in previous chapters and it is hoped here to bring these together and show how they form part of a coherent system. As was pointed out in the Introduction to this book, socialisation prepares essentially biological beings to participate in the society to which they belong and communicate with other members of that society. The social world is not an objective reality, but a perception of reality moulded by language and the rest of the symbolic order, much of which is learnt very early. It was suggested, therefore, that the first few years of life provide us with a foundation which may later be hard to recognise as culturally relative. It is this foundation with which we are here concerned.

As in Chapter II, the child's progress will be considered chronologically, as it passes through the various stages outlined there. Its experience in the three main arenas of home, neighbourhood and kindergarten or nursery will be considered in that order, although the first two of these stages will merge a little as they did in Chapters III and IV. It should also be borne in mind that an individual child may have more or less institutional life, depending on the age at which this starts, although it was emphasised by the caretakers that the atmosphere for a baby in a day nursery is made as much like home as possible. It is not necessary to attach ages to the various stages, for it will be seen that they complement one another, so that eventually children should emerge with a clear understanding of the basic categories, whatever age they moved into a wider social world than the home and immediate neighbourhood.

Early period in the home (*nyūjiki*)

Security

It seems that the chief emphasis during the first few months of a child's life is on the creation of security. This starts with the way the pregnant mother is told that her moods may affect the foetus in her uterus, so she tries to establish an appropriately calm atmosphere in which to live. Once the baby is born, this atmosphere should be upheld, where possible, and the baby should be shielded from fears and anxiety. If it cries, it is assumed to be expressing a need, even if only that of loneliness, and it is usually attended to quite swiftly. Indeed, a good mother is supposed to be able to anticipate her baby's requirements, the beginning of the art of non-verbal communication which she should later pass on to her children for dealings with other people. Early interpersonal relations include a good deal of physical contact and should be characterised by the comfort and care of the familiar and practised members of the immediate family. The stated concern is with the baby's developing emotions, which should be exposed in these early stages only to calm, security and happiness.

Once these principles have been established, the details of early care may well be rather variable and mothers may or may not feed regularly, may or may not use bottles rather than breast, may or may not buy a cot and a push-chair. The first aim is to understand the baby's patterns of expectation and form a relationship of trust with the child. The Western practices which have been rejected are perhaps more revealing than those which have been adopted. It is unlikely, for example, that a child will be given its own room, away from the rest of the family, or entrusted to relatively strange baby sitters. If a mother must work outside the home, and there is no grandparent to take care of the baby, then she will try to find one regular, individual caretaker in the immediate neighbourhood, so that the baby's home routine may be interrupted as little as possible. Even in nurseries which do accept babies under one year old, they are usually in small numbers in familiar enclosed surroundings. Ideally, however, such a baby should be in its own home surrounded by the familiar and attentive faces of its own family.

Self identity

Amongst the first words that a baby hears constantly is its own name, simplified if necessary, with the suffix *chan* added as an affectionate use of the term of respect *san*. Adults address a baby in this way from as soon as it begins to take any notice, especially since an early response – a *hai* – is praised as an accomplishment and encouraged as an important element of *shitsuke*. This indicates an awareness of being addressed, and a politeness in the response, but it also represents an ability unique to the baby to reply to its own name, important since people only a little older have an elusive knack of becoming absorbed in roles such as those of big brother and sister.

Once the baby begins to talk back, adults help, as they do in any society, but in Japan there is an early distinction to be made when the child seeks a term of self-reference, and that is the distinction between the sexes. In fact, the child may for some time use its own name instead of a personal pronoun, as is indeed the case in other languages, but Japanese boys are often addressed by the male term for I, namely *boku*. Thus, they begin to use it in reference to themselves. A little girl, on the other hand, should not use this term (although some older ones do to express ideals of equality of the sexes), and a younger sister who copies her big brother is corrected and encouraged to use the word *watashi* instead. This creates an early awareness of sex differences hard to avoid even if parents were otherwise to try and treat their boys and girls in the same way.

Other aspects of early training, reflected in other words that a baby first becomes familiar with, are concerned with bodily functions and therefore help the baby become aware of its physical self-identity. Some are concerned with feeding, some with elimination, others with activities and accomplishments such as crawling, walking, dressing, washing and bathing. In each case the training involves the gradual encouragement of self-control. A baby in any society will eventually attain the ability to take care of itself in these respects, but in most cases Japanese caretakers do not wait for these things to happen naturally. They carefully guide the child in the 'proper' way to do things, often through clearly defined physical aid, and the child learns to impose a cultural order on its physical development.

Divisions of time and space

Another way in which this cultural order is imposed at this early stage, largely through some of the same activities, is on time and space. Again, distinctions are made linguistically, but also emphasised in non-verbal ways, and there is great use of ritual. Thus the baby's life is divided into several clearly defined periods of different activity. Even if they are not placed at regular intervals during the day, as used to be thought desirable in Western manuals of baby care, the periods associated with eating, eliminating, playing, bathing and going out, are separated from other parts of the day in ritual ways. The stereotypical phrases used before and after meals are one example, and the mother and other members of the family repeat these long before they expect a child to join in. The custom of washing hands would seem to have a ritual aspect as well as a hygienic one, and it may be necessary to bring out the table for meals in houses where the same space is used for a number of different activities.

The regularity of a child's toilet training, where the mother makes use of fixed, onomatopoeic phrases and a distinctive way of holding to make clear the activity required, is another important division of time. The addition of the honorific prefix *o* to the word for urinating, as in *oshikko*, should I think be interpreted as a slight ritualisation of the activity. Certain aspects of bathing are also ritualised, and the word for bath itself is again accorded the special prefix *o*. This could be regarded as similar to the method used to ritualise the activity of clearing up after meals or after play, when *o* is added to the word *katazuke* to announce and slightly to ritualise it.[1] This ritual separation of activities divides time, and when several activities must take place in the same room it serves a similar function as do divisions of space in Western houses which allocate separate rooms to eating, sleeping, playing and so forth.

The activity of 'going out' is also surrounded in all sorts of ritual. The word with the literal meaning of 'going out', used for clothes reserved for special outings, is also offorded the honorific prefix o (*odekake*). The child is often washed before it is dressed in such special garments, hair is brushed, and then there is the doorway ritual of donning shoes and pronouncing the phrase of departure. On return, there is a different phrase, shoes are removed and the child may well be washed again. An older child is encouraged to gargle on coming in from the outside world.

Another way in which time is divided up becomes clearer as the child begins to master some of the daily greetings. These are used in the wider community and when visitors or tradespeople call, so they represent a much more universal division of time than do activities of the family. In fact, they are rather few in number and only divide the day into: an early period, when the greeting is literally 'it is early', used for the first part of the morning; a daytime period, when the greeting is literally 'this day'; and an evening period, when the greeting is literally 'this evening'. The words which correspond to 'good night' have the literal meaning of 'rest yourself' and may also be used for a midday nap, so they do not really fit into this category, although they may be used to see people off in the late evening.

Divisions of space are probably not very evident until a child begins to move about independently. It will move from room to room, or from the inside to the outside of the house before that, but it will usually be in someone's arms, or attached to their back, and the proximity of the caretaker will make unnecessary much further information about the surroundings. Perhaps it will have become aware of the distinction between the inside and the outside of the house, through the rituals of 'going out', and this will now be reinforced. As the baby begins to get about the house by itself, it will learn that there are definite limits to its freedom, and one of the most clearly defined boundaries is that marked by the space separating the normal floor level from the outside door. This often has a steep drop down to the place where shoes are left, so that if a baby approaches, it will be diverted or discouraged with the word for 'danger' (*abunai*). A similar warning or diversion will be issued if a child approaches a hot stove, a place where it might get its fingers caught, or a 'dirty' place such as the lavatory or bathroom. Thus, the distinction between areas discouraged as 'dirty' or 'dangerous' and those 'safe' for a baby to play will probably be an early one to be learnt. The space by the outside door where shoes are kept may be regarded as both dirty and dangerous if there is a steep drop down, a particularly effective deterrent (as the informant pointed out in reference to her rubbish bucket, dirty, but dangerous if the lid comes down and catches the child's fingers).

Some such divisions of space may reinforce those already discussed as dividing time. For example, the table where the food is eaten is low in Japanese houses, and rather tempting for a child to climb on to, but this is discouraged as it is 'the place where the food is eaten'. The bathroom and toilet are separated on both counts, and again the use of slippers emphasises their boundaries. The important distinction between inside and outside is also clearly included in separations based on both time and space. The division of rooms in Japanese houses is quite different from the functional ones of Western houses. This can be quite variable from one house to another in Japan, especially in the degree to which personal space is now allocated to members of the family, but there is commonly a distinction between 'formal' and 'informal' space, that is space where visitors are received, and that which is reserved for the family. Nowadays a 'Western room' with armchairs and a coffee table may be reserved for certain visitors. The baby may begin quite early to discern differences of behaviour in his or her caretakers when visitors are present, and the space where they are received will be an appropriate place to practice the greetings which form an important part of early training.

Second stage: home and neighbourhood

Danger, dirt and fear

It begins to become clear that notions of dirt and danger are helping to delineate important boundaries in the child's world view, as was anticipated in previous chapters. In contrast to the security which is fostered in the very early period, the child is now gently introduced to a new emotion, namely that of fear. The experience of having its hand drawn near to a hot place, or caught in the rubbish bin, associates unpleasantness with this new word *abunai*, and the child learns gradually to avoid things which are described as such. The use made by the mother or other caretaker of a sharp smack to warn the child away from dirt or danger introduces a further experience to be avoided, as well as aiding the child in an understanding of the boundaries of his or her own body. The need to warn children not to put small things in their mouths is likely to have a similar benefit.

Gradually, however, threats of punishment tend to be directed out of the home, to supernatural beings or strangers passing by. The dirt and danger associated with even approaching the outside door is the beginning of an important distinction which is being developed between the security and safety of the inside of the home, established by early attentiveness, and the dangers and associated fears of the outside world. These may be safely negotiated if a child remains close to its caretakers and carries out the proper rituals, so it is important for the mother to remain on the child's side in this respect. Thus, attributing possible retribution for aberrant behaviour to supernatural beings such as demons, or unknown outsiders like policemen, puts her in a position to reassure. Once that role has been clearly established, it becomes a very effective sanction for her to withdraw her usual benevolence by putting the child in a cupboard or outside the house – its haven of comfort and security.

Such a sanction must only be rarely administered to remain effective, however, and the overall importance of maintaining relations of trust and security with a child are still regarded as essential if it is to become *sunao* – compliant and co-operative. Nor must the introduction of fears and dangers be too liberal if the child is to develop self-confidence, which is why parents often complain these days that grandparents are making their children too nervous by emphasising the dangers all the time. One grandfather I observed in Kurotsuchi used the word *abunai* constantly as he went about the village with his little granddaughter, but this had the probably desired effect of ensuring that she remained close by his side. Some modern mothers have become very Western in their child-rearing practices, holding themselves back as their youngsters try out quite dangerous games, so there is quite a range of difference in the use of this aspect of training.

In any case, the development of fear is always associated with important boundaries, so that the child is quite safe if it follows the adults' directives. Thus, at the age of about three years a child is usually allowed to play outside with its friends, for by this time it will have acquired by going out with a caretaker an understanding of places to play and places to avoid. As long as it remains in the group of friends, it is possible for them to play over quite a wide area around the neighbourhood. In any case, the development of courage is another important aspect of training, as was pointed out in Chapter IV.

The classification of people

Among the first words a child usually learns to pronounce are the names of the surrounding people. In the Japanese case, many of these names in fact represent roles, such as 'mother', 'father', 'grandmother', 'grandfather', 'elder brother' and 'elder sister'. Within the family, there is nowadays a great variety not only in the composition of the group, but also in the extent to which these labels apply to specific role behaviour. It is common for the term 'father' to apply to a person who is often absent, going about the exalted business of earning money, but there are also many families where such activity is carried out by all the adult members, possibly within the same building as the home. It is also the case in many nuclear families that the mother is a young child's constant companion; elsewhere, however, despite the idea that child-rearing is ultimately the mother's responsibility, it may be the grandmother or even the grandfather who fulfils this role. It is thus even difficult to make generalisations about child care based on sex distinctions.

Also, the terminology is only person-specific in the case of the mother and father. Grandparents may live in the home, but the same terms are applied to another couple who may only be distinguished by the addition of a qualification such as a place name. The same terms may also be applied to other elderly people living in the neighbourhood. In the same way, the terms for elder brother and sister, though they may be qualified with personal names, are also applied to older children in the neighbourhood, and may even be used for other relatives such as cousins. Other adults who people the child's life may be addressed using the terms for uncle and aunt. How then does the baby make sense of all this?

Despite the overlap in the use of terminology, it is evident that a clear distinction is again made between people associated with the inside and the outside of the house. This is reinforced every time someone steps across the threshold, when the ritual phrases articulated by members of the house are quite different from those used by callers. When the latter leave, the child is encouraged to invite them to come again, quite a different phrase from that used to see off a house member. Relatives may fall into an intermediate category here, for if they come to stay they may be temporarily treated as house members in this respect, but the very irregularity of their visits will usually separate them quite clearly from the immediate family. Within the house itself, the previously mentioned division of rooms into formal and informal will help a child to distinguish visiting relatives from more casual visitors, although special occasions may well demand formal behaviour from everyone.

The members of the house thus become a clearly defined 'inside' group, distinguished ritually from others even though similar terms may be used to address them. The identity of this group is given a commonly-used term *uchi*, which literally means 'inside', though it stands for the people, belongings, customs and idiosyncracies of this entity. It is contrasted with the terms *soto*, which means outside, and *yoso*, which means 'other' in reference to other people, their belongings and customs. In a close-knit neighbourhood or community the child may also early become aware of the application of these same terms to the wider entity to which its family belongs, and thus contrasted with other neighbourhoods or communities, but this may not become clear until later when a child joins a children's group based on community membership.

The terminology in the family also distinguishes people according to generation, and eventually various forms of respect language will be learnt by children to apply to the various categories of adults they encounter. This becomes important rather later, however, and at this stage the child probably only absorbs rather unconsciously the different levels of politeness used by its parents. This change in behaviour is particularly marked as the child accompanies an adult out of the house, or when a relative stranger is received in, so the inside/outside distinction is emphasised yet again.

Terminology also distinguishes most people by gender, and there are various ways in which this distinction is reinforced. Boys and girls are usually dressed differently at home, and certainly their festive garments are quite distinct. A boy baby may wear a black garment displaying the family crest from the first presentation to the shrine, whereas a girl will wear brightly coloured garments on such occasions. For the 7–5–3 celebration, girls are often dressed in traditional kimono whereas boys are just as likely to wear little suits. 'Girls' day' and 'boys' day' each year define distinct areas of interest, and these are reinforced in the kind of toys given to children of each sex. Typically, girls' toys emphasise domestic activities with a whole range of pretty pink objects for playing house, whereas boys' toys pursue the themes of bravery and adventure, with monsters and robots being among the most popular objects.

Attitudes differ from an early stage, too, and boys are told not to cry because they are boys, and girls to sit nicely because they are girls. It used to be the case that girls and boys were even expected to sleep in different positions – girls with their legs demurely together, boys all outstretched, and one mother reported that she tidies up her daughters' legs if they are splayed out when they are sleeping. Generally, rough behaviour is tolerated much more in boys than in girls, and another mother explained that a girl should be properly trained, whereas boys are encouraged to be *nobinobi*. Nevertheless, in the early period, boys and girls play together rather well, and their games only become clearly separated when they start to go to school.

Interpersonal relations

Great emphasis is placed on harmony and happiness when small children play together, and we have seen that the method used to achieve this ideal begins to introduce the notion of hierarchy. This is where the importance of the use of the terms for 'big brother' and 'big sister' comes into play, and, as discussed in Chapter II, the responsibility and benevolence of the superior side of hierarchical relations is the one likely first to be emphasised. As soon as a quarrel develops over toys, the older child involved is encouraged to demonstrate its superior age and experience by giving in to the younger one. Privileges associated with superior age help to make the pill palatable, and possibly help to minimise sibling rivalry, since there is a fixed pecking order when each of younger and older may benefit. The same principles operate in the neighbourhood, when larger groups of children play together, and the whole group will support the ideal of benevolence from older to younger child. The linguistic distinctions made when younger children ask older ones to play, as opposed to vice versa, emphasise this, and the idea that older children are doing the younger ones the favour of looking after them emphasises their implicit obligation to help them if necessary. They are thus entrusted also with a degree of responsibility, which they seem to take rather seriously, even and perhaps especially when no adults are present.

The baby and younger child's receipt of such indulgence and care probably does no more than add to the general development of trust and security, so the first experiences of the inferior side of the hierarchical role system are likely to be those mentioned in the previous section, when respect language is expected. Part of this will be discovered while going about with a caretaker and participating in her network of relations, but the child may be specifically encouraged to use terms of respect for a grandparent. Otherwise, greetings which form an important part of early training tend to be reciprocal ones such as 'good morning', 'good day' etc., or those which are associated with entry into and exit from the home. The bow is a non-verbal expression of respect which is learnt very early, but at this stage I think it is used generally as a polite greeting, rather than as any indication of hierarchical deference.

The concept of reciprocity, implicitly evident in greetings, is consciously developed in various ways. The offering of sweets or other little treats, which we might interpret as the use of reward or even bribe, seems to be clearly linked to very specific expectations of behaviour, as was pointed out in Chapter IV. For example, the ice cream will be promised, but only given if the child goes willingly to its music lesson. As children become old enough to understand money, coins are given in exchange for specific tasks carried out, and this practice is compared with the earlier use of sweets. Such exchanges are also phrased in terms of promises (*yakusoku*), which are made very sacred by the rhyme which threatens the drinking of a thousand needles should they turn out to be a lie.

As a child gets into its third year and is deemed able to understand reason, mothers appeal to the principles of reciprocity again in exhorting them to think of others and avoid causing trouble. Thus they are encouraged to consider how they would like to receive antisocial behaviour they might be handing out, or to put themselves into the position of other people to see how they might react themselves in a certain situation. This is part of the training in non-verbal communication, and has the dual experience for the child of developing its own self-awareness in order to understand how others might feel. These principles operate too in a child's relations with adults other than those of its own family, when it is taught explicitly how to avoid causing *meiwaku* or trouble. Then the concept of obligation is also involved, and this is emphasised as children learn to say 'thank you' (*arigatō*) and hear their mothers use the expression *sumimasen,* which is a combination of 'thank you' and 'sorry'. The quite explicit connection between obligation and reciprocity will become gradually clearer to the child as it gets older, depending on its degree of involvement with its mother's network of obligations and gift exchange.

All this training in interpersonal relations is geared towards the maintenance of harmony and the congenial atmosphere parents try to create for their children. Hence, the ideal amongst children playing that they should be *nakayoku* (on good terms, at peace, harmonious), and able to play happily with anyone. This is emphasised by adults as important training for smooth social relations in later life, as was discussed in Chapter II. This is the underlying reason for the time taken to establish the source of discord when children quarrel and the great pressure put on the recalcitrant child to apologise. It is also why 'sorry' is one of the few phrases that mothers really insist that their children pronounce clearly, and the injured party must accept the apology so that a state of harmony may be restored.

Crying is no longer indulged, and once an apology has been secured, children should return to being cheerful and *nakayoku*. Indeed, a crying child is now laughed at, scorned into being 'brave' or 'strong', and adults actually encourage other children to ridicule a cry baby as *okashii* – 'strange', 'peculiar', different from the happy cheerful child who represents the ideal. The force of this insult is greater when we consider the overt ideal expressed that children should be *jūninnami* – 'ordinary', like everyone else. There is often an emphasis on sex differences again in this context as a boy, especially, is scorned for crying with phrases like 'aren't you a boy?' In extreme cases, however, adults will eventually give in to a child of either sex who is unable to achieve control, again in the interest of harmony.

Self-development

The development of the self continues in this stage, despite the emphasis on thinking of others: indeed, it is said to be through coming to understand oneself that one comes to understand others, and thus work out appropriate behaviour. The concept of individual ownership is implicit in phrases used to encourage children to lend their toys: 'It is yours,' a mother agrees when a child protests about another child picking up a toy, 'but lend it to the baby who isn't old enough to understand that yet', or 'lend it to your friend, how would you like it if he wouldn't let you play with his toys?'

Physical training also continues in the learning of the skills of eating, dressing, bathing and so on, and this is when the emphasis begins on the importance of looking after one's own things and doing things for oneself. Parents also encourage children to formulate views and express their opinions, although if they are too forceful in this respect it is seen as a problem. The aim is self-knowledge, rather than self-assertion, and an understanding must be gained of the limitations of self-interest. This is where the emphasis on avoiding being *wagamama* (selfish) becomes relevant, because a child is expected at first to be selfish, but should be trained to recognise this and control it.

Thus, by the end of the second period, the child should have achieved a fair measure of self-control. It should be capable of attending to most of its own physical needs, given the wherewithal, it should be able to express itself and make itself understood, and it should be capable of playing harmoniously with other children. Until now, it has usually had the option of returning to an attentive adult's side if social life becomes too much, but the next stage puts it firmly into a fairly formalised social world as well.

Formal social relations: kindergarten and day nursery

Friends and fun

For some weeks, or even months, before a child is ready to enter a kindergarten or day nursery, adults will try to prepare for a smooth transition to this new stage of development. The words which recur frequently in this preamble are *tomodachi* (friends) and *tanoshii* (fun). The child is said to be lucky, because it will have the chance to make lots of new friends with whom it will be able to have fun. There is no doubt about this abundance of 'friends' because of the way everyone in the class will be referred to constantly as a 'friend', so that the child has no need to make any effort in this respect. The 'friend' here is not someone you choose, or who chooses you, but is the name given to the large number of children who now share a new 'inside' group in the kindergarten or day nursery.

The characteristic of all these children, which distinguishes them from children one has known in the neighbourhood, is that they are all deemed equal in the eyes of the teacher and other adults in the establishment. Amongst themselves, the children may well know

their exact relative ages, especially when they have joined to celebrate one another's birthdays, but symbolically, at least, they are
regarded as equally entitled to the teacher's attention. Sex differences
are played down too at this stage, since the uniforms are usually the
same for boys and girls and few activities are differentiated or even
allocated on the basis of gender. In some kindergartens the forms of
address may differ – *san* for girls and *kun* for boys being added on to
their given names – but in others the suffix *chan* is still used for both
of them.

Great emphasis is laid on the 'fun' one will have at kindergarten or
day nursery. This word will be repeated again and again at the
institution itself, so that a child who is reluctant to go there, or stay
when its mother leaves, is regarded as most strange and peculiar –
okashii. It is quite inappropriate then to cry at such a place and if a
child fails to control itself in the early stages, the teachers may
encourage it to come and enjoy itself. Most caretakers expect to
spend about a week at the beginning of each new year giving special
attention to the new children. If crying persists, however, the child
will probably find itself ignored, as the teacher must attend to the
important matter of making life *tanoshii* for all the other children in
the class. There is really nothing for a reluctant child to do but to join
in and have fun with the others. It may take some time, but since little
attention is paid to a crying child, it eventually learns to gain the
self-control required.

Of course, day nurseries which accept babies and tiny children
must make allowances for the lack of home training to prepare them
for this stage of development, and this is possible in classes with
smaller numbers. Babies are not given quite the attention they would
receive with an individual caretaker, but they are usually so few in
number that they can be given quite a lot of personal care. There are
plenty of toys to amuse them as they get a little older, and enough
adults to intervene if they have troubles with their playmates. Sometimes the nursery nurses will move with their babies into the next
classes to provide continuity until they reach about the third year
when they are thought to be ready to mingle with groups of larger
numbers.

Divisions of time and space

One of the ways in which training is rather similar whether it be at home or in a kindergarten or day nursery is in the ritual divisions made of time and space. Here, too, the periods associated with eating, eliminating, playing, clearing-up, and now study of different kinds are separated from one another by the use of ritual phrases and, this time, tunes on the piano or organ. Hand-washing and changing may also be involved, as they are at home. Here, too, space is divided ritually with the use of tables, marking tape, mattresses, or the children themselves, in order to separate off various activities from others during the day. Thus, the empty space where the children gather in the morning may be filled with tables for drawing and handicrafts, emptied again for musical movement, filled with tables again for lunch, emptied and laid out with mattresses for rest-time, and cleared up for the end of the day.

The most important new rituals of this sort are those which initiate and end the day at kindergarten or nursery, and these seem to have an important role of defining the group as it gathers each day. The rituals of changing shoes and clothes on arrival are similar to those practised at the entrance to the home, and mark the inside of the classroom off from the rest of the world. Again, the inside is associated with the group which gathers there and the fun they have together so that it is appropriate that a child who is reluctant to join in may stand alone outside. The children often play outside, or attend special classes in other rooms, but they go together on these occasions. Thus, the threat for a child who misbehaves to be sent out alone is a very effective one. As at home, the inside is made secure and attractive, this time with the concept of 'fun', so that the outside can be effectively opposed as an unattractive and strange place to want to be.

New divisions of time may be emphasised now that days of the week take on a different character depending on whether a day is a whole or half kindergarten or nursery day, or a holiday one. There is also the division of each appropriate day into time to be spent at home and time to be spent in such an establishment. Larger divisions of time such as months and years are also becoming established as cyclical in the child's scheme of things, although this may have started at home with celebrations of annual events such as birthdays, New Year, and other festivals, discussed in Chapter I. The idea of the progression of time should also become clear at this stage as the children move up through the classes of kindergarten or day nursery. As well as the ritual distinction of the class from the outside world, there are also events which help to make clear the identity of the whole kindergarten or nursery as a unit. These are probably almost universally the birthday parties which take place monthly or less frequently, termly assemblies, and annual events such as sports day, concerts and the graduation ceremony.

Collective identity

The chief object and new experience of these establishments is to introduce the child to *shūdan seikatsu* (group life) in preparation for subsequent entry to school. As well as being defined spatially and temporally in ritual ways already mentioned, there are several other ways in which the concept of the collective is inculcated into the children. These include the way the child who has been much fussed over as an individual now finds itself among a large number of other children, all equally important in the teacher's eyes, emphasised in the way children wear identical uniforms and have identical sets of equipment. Much of the time they may also be engaged in identical activities, although these could also be part of a co-operative effort, made by the class as a whole. This entity of the whole class is referred to and addressed by the teacher as the personalised collective *mina-san*. The same term may be used for the whole kindergarten, and a sense of responsibility for its property is instilled by means of applying the concept of ownership to this collective unit. Children are exhorted to take care of things 'because they belong to *mina-san*'.

Co-operation should characterise behaviour within this group, and the aim should again be harmonious interaction. As far as possible the adults encourage the children to put pressure on each other to co-operate in the activities arranged for them, so that stragglers are urged to pull themselves together for the sake of the whole class. It seems that this is a very effective method of gaining willing co-operation among the children, but the ideals of co-operation are also advocated in the stories and television programmes which constantly reiterate the theme that co-operation can achieve so much more than individual endeavour. The Japanese version of the English story of Three Little Pigs illustrates this point very well, since it is a direct example of the modification of something Western to suit Japanese requirements.

Collective identity is also expressed in the class co-operative efforts pinned up on the wall, such as the sea full of individually fashioned fishes, the wood full of trees, or a train full of people. Whatever the theme, the children have each contributed to a grand creation to decorate their classroom walls. Meals are usually taken in the individual classrooms rather than in a school hall. Music and singing classes involve a good measure of singing in unison, and may gradually introduce the idea of harmony to the children as well. The ultimate in this direction was the eighty-piece orchestra organised for the children in their last year at Shirayuri Kindergarten. This group also rehearsed an impressive drumming display for the annual sports day. It was on this occasion too that the value placed on co-operative activity was witnessed by a long line of parents pointing cameras at the grand tug-of-war. In Kumamoto, the hundreds of children who attend Kyushu Music Kindergarten put on a complicated marching display, which has them creating tableaux and forming words, an event often televised and certainly attended by a large audience.

The duty system within the class also introduces a child to a rather democratic distribution of roles which could, taken out of context, be interpreted as hierarchical. Each child takes a turn to serve, discipline and represent the others, so that each child also experiences all sides of this interaction. Thus, when a child is asked to do something by another whose role he or she will also have to play, he co-operates in the hope that others will co-operate when it is his turn. This principle continues into school, and no doubt provides good preparation for participation later in actual hierarchical roles within a work situation. This equitable distribution of 'hierarchical roles', as well as the importance placed on age when everyone grows old eventually, may well explain why the Japanese form of hierarchy appears to be so much more palatable than the traditional Western type currently does.

Interpersonal relations

Other manifestations of hierarchical principles continue in interpersonal relations in the institutional setting since children have plenty of time for free play, inside and outside, as well as for organised activities. Usually children in the same class, who are in principle equal, know well each other's ages for interaction in the playground, which then follows similar rules to that in the neighbourhood, although physical strength and force of character may well have parts to play here too. Certainly relations between children in different classes follow the age lines, and there is a kind of collective hierarchy amongst the classes of different ages at gatherings of the whole kindergarten or day nursery.

The relations between the class and its teacher, or between the individual pupil and the teacher, are considered ideal ones for introducing the deferential linguistic forms. Even the teacher herself may correct children who address her or refer to her in a disrespectful way, and parents should certainly do this. Similarly, at this stage, children's relations with their grandparents and other appropriate adults become a little more formal and respectful as they learn the speech forms required. Interviews usually reported that they made little active effort to teach polite forms to kindergarten children, but if a child used disrespectful language, they would correct them with the appropriate form. Thus small children begin to conceive of the generational differences and the hierarchical notions associated with them. This is probably also the stage at which girls' and boys' language begins to differ. Boys are allowed to get away with all sorts of vulgar speech forms, especially amongst themselves, but mothers begin to guide their daughters into the more respectful, feminine forms.

The self in the collective

Finally, it should be reiterated that a child does not disappear as an individual into this new collective entity. In the last chapter, it was noted that Piaget had pointed out the greater effectiveness of mutual co-operation, rather than unilateral constraint to regulate children's behaviour. He writes that it is 'the essence of democracy to replace the unilateral respect of authority by the mutual respect of the autonomous wills'.[2] Co-operation, then, far from denying the development of personhood, actually implies autonomy, or, in Piaget's view, 'personalities that are both conscious of themselves and able to submit their point of view to the laws of reciprocity and universality'.[3] This is precisely what is overtly sought by Japanese parents entering their children into kindergarten – self-awareness sufficient for the understanding of others, self-knowledge in the interest of maintaining harmonious social relations. As Durkheim pointed out long ago in *L'Education Morale,* 'the attachment to social groups . . . far from checking individual initiative . . . enriches personality'.[4]

Raum argued a similar point based on his observations of Chaga children. He takes issue with Rousseau's idea that the *amour de soi* or the 'tendency towards the unfolding of the self in a spontaneous manner' is opposed to and restrained by the relations of social life. Raum argues that juvenile spontaneity does not work itself out *in vacuo* but defines itself by reference to the cultural environment. He argues therefore that individual nature and society are not at educational poles: 'Society exists only in individuals and individuals realise themselves only in society'.[5]

The children spend long hours with each other, especially in a day nursery, and they come to know each member of the group very well. During the course of the day, the teacher also picks out individuals for praise and reproach; representatives have to be chosen for races at sports day or special performances in concerts; and there is also time for children to speak in front of the class about their own personal experiences and thoughts on particular incidents and events. Each child has a set of personal property, albeit identical to all the others', but the responsibility for its care lies with the owner. The teacher also has the benefit of a detailed personal form filled out by the parents for each member of her class, and she visits all their homes soon after they arrive at the start of the year.

As well as experiencing 'group life', children in these establishments are also expected to develop qualities of character such as perseverance and effort, independence and self-reliance, 'creative expression' and the ability to know and express one's own mind. These and individual talents may be further developed in smaller private classes of the type described in Chapter II. Particularly in sports and dancing classes, but anyway in most pre-school establishments, there is still plenty of chance to pursue the development of bodily awareness and training of physical control. Outside classes, too, mothers will continue to demonstrate the proper way to sit, stand and bow in particular situations, and the child will gradually be expected to become more and more proficient in these arts. After all, the aspect of *shitsuke* concerning the 'beautification of the body' has not been forgotten.

Thus, children in the third stage come to develop in a new sense as members of a group whose identity they learn to appreciate, and for whose benefit they realise they must sometimes control their own personal interests. Through such training they achieve a new identity of their own as members belonging to, co-operating in, and enjoying the benefits of a collective organisation. This gives them an important extra dimension in which to operate, a dimension which is less developed in the West, and I suggest that it is because of this lack that we may tend to lose out in some of Befu's 'cultural cues' (p. 2). For, as several anthropologists and linguists have pointed out, although the terminology I borrow here is that of Basil Bernstein, the closer the identifications of speakers, and the greater the range of shared interests, the more restricted and predictable is the speech they employ. Much of the intent of communication can be taken for granted so there is less need to raise meanings to the level of explicitness, or what Bernstein terms elaboration. Thus a speaker wishing to individualise his communication, Bernstein argues, is likely to do it by varying the expressive associates of the speech, so that more concern may be found with how something is said and when, its metaphoric elements, and the interpretation of silence. The unspoken assumptions are not available to outsiders.[6]

We are all probably aware of this type of communication in close personal relationships, but socialisation in Western societies seems to involve variable amounts of experience in interpreting non-verbal cues, which are anyway picked up in a much less self-conscious manner. It is rather the elaborated speech code which is emphasised, particularly in middle-class families, according to Bernstein, who sees the English education system as difficult for children whose family background has given them a more restricted, though just as acceptable, speech code. In Japan, where speech is often quite accurately predictable, and thus 'restricted' in Bernstein's sense, meaning in relationships must often be sought elsewhere. Early socialisation in anticipating the needs of others through self-awareness, reciprocity in inter-personal relationships, and the experience of group identity, provides a firm basis for skill in this respect.

The 'fun' of the pre-school establishment is no mythical ideal which exists only in the words of teachers and parents. It is plainly evident in the faces and attitudes of the children who run each day to join their playmates in their own particular classroom. I suggest it also forms the foundation for the satisfaction found later by adults who apparently willingly put the demands of the work place before their own conflicting personal interest.

Some structural principles

It seems possible to summarise some of the important aspects of a child's early upbringing by drawing up a series of oppositions which seem to emerge as important in the system of classification being presented. Since they are based on an analysis of the total symbolic system, the elements of this scheme may or may not be emphasised consciously by the adults involved, but they are anyway implicit in their approach to small children. They also seem on the whole to underly the most diverse range of detailed treatment.

First of all, there is an opposition set up in the early years between the security and trust of the inside of the home and dangers and associated fears of the outside world. It is not a completely clear-cut distinction, since there may be dangers in the home, and the outside world is made safe as long as certain conditions are fulfilled, but the clustering of associations would seem to support the scheme:

Security (*Anshin*)   Danger (*Abunai*)
Trust (*Shinrai*)   Fear (*Shinpai*)
Inside (*Uchi*)   Outside (*Soto*)
Family (*Kazoku*)   Others (*Yoso no hito*)

It is especially apt when we recall that the Japanese term *uchi* refers not only to the inside of the house, but also to the people who belong to that group, so that if one goes outside with members of that group the distinction is anyway blurred somewhat. It is also with these people that one's relations of trust are first established and one's fears allayed in a situation of potential danger. However, there are others, possibly close relatives or neighbours at first, in whom children are gradually also encouraged to place their trust, and the outside world becomes more manageable as the child grows up a little and begins to experience other 'inside' groups, such as the neighbourhood and kindergarten.

The first simple set of oppositions widens out then to incorporate a larger group of friends, relatives and potential caretakers, and a larger number of principles come into operation in interpersonal and collective behaviour with these people. The principles first established in the neighbourhood seem to be reinforced more formally in kindergartens and day nurseries, and it seems possible to draw up another set of oppositions based on the ideals of behaviour and their alternatives:

Cheerful child (*Akarui*)	Cry baby (*Nakimushi*)
Harmony (*Nakayoku*)	Quarrels (*Kenka*)
Having fun (*Tanoshii*)	Strange (*Okashii*)
Like others (*Jūninnami*)	Peculiar (*Okashii*)
Compliance	Ridicule
Belonging	Left-out
Co-operation	Ostracism
Inside	Outside

The alternatives are discouraged at first, as the opposite of the ideals, and the Japanese words given are used in these contexts, but as one proceeds down the list, the alternatives become so unpleasant that there becomes less and less need for discouragement and the oppositions represent my interpretations of behaviour. In fact, there is really no alternative at all. Ultimately, it is not a matter of co-operating with the group or being individualistic, as a Western view might represent things:[7] it's rather co-operation or being left out, being happy like every one else or being laughed at, a choice between compliance and ostracism. The only alternative to joining in at kindergarten is to stand outside, either because one has not yet summoned up the self-control to participate, or because one has been sent there for interrupting the harmony of the class. It's a matter of being one of the group, or being nothing at all. In the end it is not really a choice. It's the way of the world.

A parallel set of oppositions which is being developed is that concerning the relationship between the self and the rest of the world. Child-training has gradually made it possible for the individual child to define itself as a discrete identity, but it also teaches it about the control it must exercise over the will and behaviour of this being. Although the difference has probably not yet been clearly articulated, it will eventually learn that there is behaviour appropriate for the outside world and behaviour appropriate for the various groups to which it belongs. In fact, the self is becoming a complicated being with a face and appropriate behaviour for each of the arenas in which it operates.[8] It is evident when one listens carefully to the different speech forms used when a child converses with its mother, its age-mates, children slightly older, its teacher, complete strangers and so on. These distinctions may be made by a child in any society, but in Japan they are being institutionalised, and foundations for the institutionalisation have been very firmly laid. Again, we seem to return to the important basic distinction between the inside and the outside, this time that of the individual being:

Self (*Jibun*)	Others (*Hoka no hito*)
Selfish (*Wagamama*)	Kind, thoughtful (*Yasashii, Omoiyari*)
Own thoughts and feelings (*Honne, Kokoro, Hara*)	Face shown to the world (*Tatemae, Kao, Kuchi*)

In this case the inside and outside of the individual being is distinguished, and as may be seen in the last line, there are various Japanese words used to refer to the inside self as opposed to the 'face' shown to the world. These are translated in various ways, including 'private' and 'public', 'informal' and 'formal', and more literally for the second and third of each set, 'heart' and 'face', 'belly' and 'mouth'.[9] The outside must be flexible enough to accommodate various situations within groups and in the wider outside world too. In all cases there is an appropriate way to behave. The family is traditionally the unit in which the individual should be able to be closest to his or her own inside core, but here too there are others to consider in order to maintain harmony in interpersonal relations.

Finally, the mechanisms by which these ideals are approached and their opposites avoided involve various, more complex classificatory principles. There is the notion of hierarchy, which is experienced in a most palatable way since the superior side is introduced before the inferior one – quite the reverse of the Western situation where a child must often wonder if it will ever gain a position of any consequence. It is also different since the emphasis is on responsibility and benevolence, rather than power. Then, there are the notions of reciprocity and obligation, which operate in several different spheres. The ideas of equality and democracy in the strictest sense are firmly established in kindergarten, where co-operation is achieved not by directives from above, but by drawing out the apparently natural propensity of children to make rules among themselves. A glance at almost any work on adult activities in Japan will confirm the later importance of all these principles, although there has been a tendency to focus on that which contrasts with the West. It is hoped that here a more complex picture has been presented of how early and how effectively these underlying principles are learnt.

Notes

1   A detailed discussion of usages of the honorific prefix *o* is to be found in Miller 1980: 276–81, although he does not comment on ritual usage.
2   Piaget 1932: 366.
3   *Ibid.* 372.
4   *Ibid.* 356.
5   Raum 1940: 386.
6   Bernstein 1974.
7   Befu 1980.
8   Cf. Kumon 1982: 16–17.
9   Lebra 1976: 159–60.

Appendix

Part I: Interview families

M = mother; F = father; g = grand; D = daughter; S = son

Family Occupation	Mother		Abode	Children
A F ship surveyor	M at home	nuclear	Yokohama	1D 1S
B F driver	M at home	nuclear	Tateyama	1D
C F business gF/gM various	M at home	continuing	Tateyama	3S
D Family business	incl. M	continuing	Tateyama	2S
E Family business	incl. M	continuing	Tateyama	2S 1D
F Family business	incl. M	continuing	Miyoshi	2S 1D
G Farming family	incl. M	continuing	Miyoshi	1S 1D
H F Hitachi employee	M at home	nuclear	Chiba	2S
I F Public employee gM/gF artisans	M at home	continuing	Tateyama	1S 1D
J Family business	M at home	nuclear	Tateyama	3D
K Doctors' family	M helps	nuclear flat cont. building	Tateyama	3S
L Family inn F employed	M at home	nuclear house next door to inn	Tateyama	1S 2D
L* Family business	incl. M	nuclear house in cont. compound	Tateyama	1D 2S
M F employed	M teacher	nuclear	Tateyama	2S
N F kindergarten teacher	M occasional help at kindergarten	nuclear	Tateyama	2S
O F nursery nurse	M teacher	nuclear	Tateyama	1S 1D
P F salesman gF lecturer	M teacher (part time)	continuing	Tateyama	1D
Q F sailor	M at home	nuclear	Tateyama	1D 1S
R F carpenter	M/gM sewing	continuing	Tateyama	2D

Family Occupation	Mother		Abode	Children
S	F artisan	M in office	nuclear	Tateyama	1S
T	F English teacher	M teacher (occasional)	nuclear	Tokyo	1S 1D
U	F psychiatrist	M teacher (occasional)	nuclear	Tateyama	2D
V	F psychiatrist	M at home	nuclear (family hosp.)	Tateyama	1S
W	F salesman	M office gM childcare	extended	Tateyama	1S 1D
X	F employee	M office	nuclear	Tateyama	1S
Y	F train driver	M office	nuclear home contin. line	Tateyama	1S 1D
Z	Family retail trade	incl. M	nuclear	Tateyama	4S
Ak	F public employee	M at home	nuclear	Fukuoka	1D 1S
Bk	F/gF employed	M employed gM at home	continuing	Kurotsuchi	1D 1S
Ck	Family business	M at home	nucleàr home (cont. bus.)	Kyushu	2D 1S
Dk	F carpenter	M at home	nuclear	Kurotsuchi	2S
Ek	F employed gM sewing at home	M teacher (occasional)	continuing	Kyushu	2D 1S
Fk	Farming family	incl. M	continuing	Kurotsuchi	2D 1S
Gk	F employed gF/gM farm	M at home	continuing	Kurotsuchi	2D
Hk	F carpenter	M/gM/gF farm	continuing	Kurotsuchi	1S
Ik	Farming family	gF childcare	continuing	Kurotsuchi	2D 1S
Jk	Farming family	incl. M	continuing	Kurotsuchi	1S
Kk	Farming family	incl. M	continuing	Kurotsuchi	3S
Lk	F employed Family business	M at home	continuing	Kurotsuchi	1D
Mk	Farming family	incl. M	continuing	Kurotsuchi	1S
Nk	F public employee gM artisan	M at home	continuing	Kurotsuchi	2D.
Ok	Family business	incl. M	continuing	Kurotsuchi	1D
Pk	Farming family	incl. M	continuing	Kurotsuchi	2S 2D
Qk	Farming family	incl. M	continuing	Kurotsuchi	2S 1D
Rk	F employed	M at home	nuclear	Kurotsuchi	2D
Sk	F employed	M employed gM at home	continuing	Kurotsuchi	1D
Tk	Farming family	incl. M	continuing	Kurotsuchi	2S
Uk	Farming family	gF childcare	continuing	Kurotsuchi	1D
Vk	Farming family	gF childcare	continuing	Kurotsuchi	2D 1S
Wk	F employed gM farming	M sewing (part-time)	continuing	Kurotsuchi	2S 1D

Part II: Questions put to the interview families

These questions were asked in an informal manner to leave open the possibility of diversion should a new or particularly interesting topic emerge. If the questions were not completed in one session, it was usually possible to arrange a second one, although since I saw most of the mothers involved quite frequently there was also the possibility of clarifying points left unfinished or obscure later. The interviews were usually carried out in the home of the interviewee, or in my home, sometimes while our children played around us. We were thus interrupted from time to time, but we also had the possibility of bringing the children into the discussion. The presence or otherwise of the children seemed to make little difference to the answers (whereas I suspect it might have in England), but if a father appeared he tended to take over the interview from his wife and bring the discussion onto a more theoretical than pracitical level. It was also occasionally more appropriate to ask the questions of a grandmother since the mother was out at work, but I always spoke also to the mother.

The following list includes the areas covered.

1   Composition of family and occupations. Where the mother is from.
2-5 Celebrations held for children (all those discussed in chapter I were named).
6   Daily routine of babies and children including
7   toilet training and
8   sleeping arrangements.
9   Important aspects of *shitsuke*.
10 Division of labour in the family.
11 What presents are given? When?
12 What kind of person would you like your child to become?
13 What makes you cross with the children?
14 For what things do you praise them?

15 Do you punish them? If so, how? Do you use threats? If so, what kind?
16 Do you reward them? If so, how? (Linked with 11.)
17 Does the father have a special role? If so, what?
18 Does anyone teach the children to read? What else do you teach them?
19 Do the children go to classes? If so, which?
20 Are they involved in neighbourhood activities?
21 Do they receive pocket money?
22 Do you teach them respect language? When is this taught?

Part III: Questionnaire circulated to the parents of Shirayuri Kindergarten

---

Age and Sex of Child
1. Whether can read or write?
2. Who taught them?
3. Is anything else taught at home?
4. Does your child take any classes outside? If so, what?
5. Please name three aspects of your current child training (*shitsuke*) which you think particularly important.

This short questionnaire was designed for the specific purpose of making up for questions lacking in the form filled in by parents entering their children into Shirayuri Kindergarten which did however appear on the one at Tateyama Kindergarten. The question about *shitsuke* was also included to help me draw up some characteristics of and categories within this wide-ranging concept. The answers are discussed in the text of the book.

Bibliography

Aberle, David F. 1961. Culture and Socialization. In Hsu, ed., *Psychological Anthropology*. Homewood, Illinois: The Dorsey Press

Ammar, Hamed. 1954. *Growing Up in an Egyptian Village: Silwa, Province of Aswan*. London: Routledge & Kegan Paul

Aoi, Kazuo *et al. c* 1970. Comparative Study of Home Discipline. In Hill & König

—— 1976. *Shitsuke Kenkyū e no Shakaigakuteki Apurōchi* (*A Sociological Approach to Research on Child-Rearing*). In Matsubara & Sato

Bachnik, Jane M. 1983. 'Recruitment strategies for household succession: rethinking Japanese household organization'. *Man* (NS) 18: 160–82

Bacon, Alice Mabel. 1891. *Japanese Girls and Women*. London: Gay & Bird

Barnlund, Dean C. 1975. Communication Styles in Two Cultures: Japan and the U.S. In Kendon *et al.*, eds., *Organization of Behavior in Face-to-Face Interaction*. The Hague and Paris: Mouton

Beauchamp, Edward R. 1978. *Learning to be Japanese*. Haunden, Connecticut: Linnet Books

Beardsley, Richard K. *et al.* 1969. *Village Japan*. Chicago University Press, Phoenix Edition

Befu, Harumi. 1971. *Japan, An Anthropological Introduction*. San Francisco: Chandler Publishing Co.

—— 1980. 'A critique of the group model in Japanese society'. *Social Analysis* 5–6: 29–43

Benedict, Ruth. 1946, rept. 1977. *The Chrysanthemum and the Sword*. London: Routledge & Kegan Paul

Bernstein, Basil. 1974. *Class, Codes and Control: Vol. I Theoretical Studies Towards a Sociology of Language*. London: Routledge & Kegan Paul

Brown, Judith K. 1975. Socialization: A Brief Review of Directions of Research. In Williams, T. R., ed.

Casal, V. A. 1967. *The Five Sacred Festivals of Ancient Japan*. Tokyo: Tuttle & Sophia University

Caudill, William & David W. Plath. 1966. 'Who sleeps by whom? Parent–child involvement in urban Japanese families'. *Psychiatry* 29: 344–66

Caudill, William & Helen Weinstein. 1969. 'Maternal care and infant behaviour in Japan and America'. *Psychiatry* 32: 12–43

Clark, Rodney. 1979. *The Japanese Company*. New Haven and London: Yale University Press

Clausen, John A., ed. 1968. *Socialization and Society*. Boston: Little, Brown & Co.

Connor, John. 1977. *Tradition and Change in Three Generations of Japanese Americans*. Chicago: Nelson-Hall

Cummings, William K. 1980. *Education and Equality in Japan*. Princeton University Press

Deasey, Denison. 1978. *Education Under Six*. London: Croom Helm

De Vos, George. 1973. *Socialization for Achievement: Essays on the Cultural Psychology of the Japanese*. Berkeley: University of California Press

Doi, Takeo. 1973a. *The Anatomy of Dependence*. trans. John Bester. Tokyo: Kodansha

—— 1973b. 'Omote and ura: concepts derived from the Japanese two-fold structure of consciousness'. *Journal of Nervous and Mental Diseases* 157, 4: 258–61

Dore, R. P. 1965. *Education in Tokugawa Japan*. Berkeley: University of California Press

—— 1971. *City Life in Japan*. Berkeley: University of California Press

—— 1973. *British Factory-Japanese Factory*. Berkeley: University of California Press

—— 1976. *The Diploma Disease*. London: George Allen & Unwin

—— 1978. *Shinohata: A Portrait of a Japanese Village*. London: Allen Lane

Douglas, Mary. 1970. *Purity and Danger: An Analysis of Concepts of Pollution and Taboo*. Harmondsworth: Penguin Books

Draguns, Juris G. 1979. Culture and Personality. In Marsella *et al*. *Perspectives on Cross-Cultural Psychology*. New York: Academic Press

Dykstra, Yoshiko Kurata. 1978. 'Jizō, the most merciful'. *Monumenta Nipponica* 33, 2: 179–200

Early Childhood Education of Japan, ed. 1979. *Early Childhood Education and Care in Japan*. Tokyo: Child Honsha

Economic Welfare Bureau (Japan). 1980. *Current State and Future Problems of the Japanese Household – Outline*. Economic Planning Agency Publication (February)

Elkind, David. 1979. *The Child and Society*. New York: Oxford University Press

Ervin-Tripp, Susan. 1977. Wait for Me, Roller-Skate. In Ervin-Tripp & Mitchell-Kernan

Ervin-Tripp, Susan & Claudia Mitchell-Kernan. 1977. *Child Discourse*. New York: Academic Press

Fujisaki, Hiro. 1957. *Kankonsōsai Jiten (Dictionary of Ceremonial)*. Tokyo: Tsuru Shobō

Fukutake, Tadashi. 1972. *Japanese Rural Society*, trans. R. P. Dore. London: Cornell University Press

—— 1976. *Kazoku to Ningenkeisei (Family and Character Formation)*. In Matsubara and Sato

Gorer, Geoffrey. 1962. Themes in Japanese Culture. In Silberman, ed.

Halliday, M. A. K. 1975. *Learning How to Mean: Explorations in the*

Development of Language. London: Arnold

Hara, Hiroko. 1980. The childhood in Japanese society during the past 100 years. Paper presented at Kolloquium 'Kindheit, Familie und Poesie im Kulturvergleich'. Goethe-Institut, Kyoto

Hara, Hiroko & Wagatsuma Hiroshi. 1974. *Shitsuke (Child-Rearing)*. Tokyo: Kōbundo

Helvoort, Ernest van. 1979. *The Japanese Working Man*. Tenterden, Kent: Paul Norbury

Hendry, Joy. 1981. *Marriage in Changing Japan*. London: Croom Helm

—— 1982. 'Teaching about childhood using ethnographic material'. *Social Science Teacher* 11, 3: 68–70

—— 1984. Shoes: the early learning of an important distinction in Japanese society. In Daniels, ed. *Europe Interprets Japan*. Tenterden, Kent: Paul Norbury Publications

Hess, Robert *et al.* 1980. 'Maternal expectations for mastery of development tasks in Japan and the United States'. *International Journal of Psychology* 15: 259–71

Hill R. & R. König, eds. *c*.1970. *Families in East and West: Socialization Process and Kinship Ties*. The Hague and Paris: Mouton

Hirai, Nobuyoshi. 1977. *Boseiai no Kaifuku no tame no Doryoku ni tsuite (Efforts to Restore Mother-Love)*. In Yoda, ed.

Hoikuen no Shiori (Day Nursery Handbook). N.d. Tateyama-City

Hsu, Francis L. K., ed. 1961. *Psychological Anthropology*. Homewood, Illinois: Dorsey Press

—— 1972. *Psychological Anthropology*. (new edition). Cambridge, Mass: Schenkman

Hubert, Jane. 1974. Belief and Reality: Social Factors in Pregnancy and Childbirth. In M. P. M. Richards, ed.

Ibuka, Masaru. 1976. *Yōchien de wa Ososugiru (It's too Late at Kindergarten)*. Tokyo: Goma Books

Inoguchi, Shoji. 1962. *Tanjō to Ikuji (Childbirth and Childcare)* and *Yōshonenki (Childhood and Adolescence)*. In Omachi *et al.*, eds.

Inouye, Jukichi. 1910. *Home Life in Tokyo*. Tokyo.

Ishiguro, Kazuo. 1982. *A Pale View of the Hills*. Harmondsworth: Penguin

Johnson Thomas W. 1975. *Shonendan: Adolescent Peer Group Socialization in Rural Japan*. Asian Folklore & Social Life Monograph No. 68. The Chinese Association for Folklore

Kenkyūsha. 1954. *New Japanese English Dictionary*.

Kerlinger, Fred N. 1962. Behaviour and Personality in Japan: A Critique of Three Studies of Japanese Personality. In Silberman, ed.

Kiefer, Christine Weber. 1970. 'The psychological interdependence of family, school and bureaucracy in Japan'. *American Anthropologist* 72,1: 66–75

Kimura, Yuko. 1981. Reading and Writing in English and Japanese Children: a Cross-Cultural Study. Oxford University D. Phil thesis

Kojima, Hideo. 1983. *Rekishiteki ni mita waga kuni no jidō hattatsukan*

(*Our country's view of child development, from a historical point of view*). In Nagano Shigefumi and Akina Yoda, eds., *Haha to Ko no Deai* (*Mother-Child Encounter*). Tokyo: Shinyōsha

Kondo, Sumio. 1974. 'Off we go to our lessons'. *Japan Interpreter* 9: 15–24

Koschmann, J. Victor. 1974. 'The idiom of contemporary Japan VIII: Tatemae to Honne'. *Japan Interpreter* 9: 98–104

Koyano, Shogo. 1964. 'Changing family behaviour in four Japanese communities'. *Journal of Marriage and the Family* 26: 149–59

Kumon, Shumpei. 1982. 'Some principles governing the thought and behaviour of Japanists (contextualists)'. *Journal of Japanese Studies* 8: 1

Kuroyanagi, Tetsuko. 1981. *Madogiwa no Totto-chan*. Tokyo: Kodansha
—— 1982. *The Little Girl at the Window* trans. D. Britten. Kodansha

La Barre, Weston. 1962. Some Observations on Character Structure in the Orient. In Silberman, ed.

Lanham, Betty. 1956. Aspects of Child Care in Japan: Preliminary Report. In D. C. Haring ed., *Personal Character and Cultural Milieu*. New York: Syracuse University Press
—— 1966. 'The psychological orientation of the mother-child relationship'. *Monumenta Nipponica* 21: 322–33

Lebra, Takie Sugiyama. 1976. *Japanese Patterns of Behaviour*. Honolulu: University Press of Hawaii

Leis, Philip. 1972. *Enculturation and Socialization in an Ijaw Village*. New York: Holt, Rinehart and Winston

Levy, Robert L. 1973. *The Tahitians*. University of Chicago Press

Lock, Margaret M. 1980. *East Asian Medicine in Urban Japan*. Berkeley: University of California Press

Makino, Tatsumi, *et al.* 1970. Juvenile Delinquency and Home Training. In Hill and König

Mama Wakatte Ne (You Understand Don't You Mummy) 1981. Chibaken Kyoikuiinkai (Chiba Prefecture Education Department)

Manabe, Kosai. 1960. *Jizō Bosatsu no Kenkyū (Research about the Bodhisatva Jizō)*. Kyoto: Fuzanbo Shoten

Maretzki, Thomas W. & Hatsumi. 1963. Taira, an Okinawan Village. In Beatrice Whiting, *Six Cultures*. New York and London: John Wiley & Sons

Matsubara, Jirō and Katsuko Satō. 1976. *Shitsuke* ('Child-rearing'). *Gendai no Esupuri (The Spirit of Today)* No. 113. Tokyo: Shibundo

Matsuda, Michio. 1973. *Nihonshiki Ikujihō (The Japanese Way of Child-rearing)*. Tokyo: Kodansha

Mayer, Philip, ed. 1970. *Socialization: The Approach from Social Anthropology*. Association of Social Anthropologists Monograph 8. Tavistock

Mead, Margaret & Martha Wolfenstein, eds. 1955. *Childhood in Contemporary Cultures*. University of Chicago Press

Menpes, Dorothy & Mortimer. 1905. *Japan: A Record in Colour*. London: Charles Black.

Middleton, John, ed. 1970. *From Child to Adult: Studies in the Anthropology of Education*. American Museum Sourcebooks in Anthropology. New York: The Natural History Press.

Miller, Roy Andrew. 1967. *The Japanese Language*. University of Chicago Press

Minear, Richard H. 1980. 'The wartime studies of Japanese national character'. *Japan Interpreter* 13: 36–59

Ministry of Foreign Affairs (Japan) Information Bulletin. 1976. Report from the Japanese Side of the World: Fertility Survey

Ministry of Health and Welfare (Japan). 1979. White paper (in Japanese)

—— 1979. A Brief Report of Child Welfare Services in Japan. Children and Families Bureau

Mitford, A. B. 1966. *Tales of Old Japan*. Tokyo: Tuttle

Miyamoto Musashi. 1982. *A Book of Five Rings,* trans. Victor Harris. London: Allison & Busby

Moloney, James Clark. 1962. Child training and Japanese conformity. In Silberman, ed.

Nakane, Chie. 1967. *Kinship and Economic Organization in Rural Japan.* L.S.E. Monographs on Social Anthropology No. 32. London: Athlone

Newson, John & Elizabeth. 1974. Cultural aspects of child-rearing in the English-speaking world. In M. P. M. Richards, ed.

Ohnuki-Tierney, Emiko. 1984. *Illness and Culture in Contemporary Japan: An Anthropological View.* Cambridge University Press

Omachi, Tokuzo *et al.* eds. 1962. *Nihon Minzokugaku Taikei (An Outline of Japanese Folklore).* Vol. 4. Tokyo: Heibonsha

Otsuka Minzokugakkai. 1979. *Nihon Minzoku Jiten (Japanese Dictionary of Folklore).* Tokyo: Kōbundo

Norbeck, Edward. 1954. *Takashima: A Japanese Fishing Community.* Salt Lake City: University of Utah Press

—— and Margaret Norbeck. 1956. Child Training in a Japanese Fishing Community. In D. G. Haring, ed., *Personal Character and Cultural Milieu.* Syracuse, New York: Syracuse University Press

—— and George De Vos. 1961. Japan. In Hsu, ed.

Piaget, J. 1932. *The Moral Judgement of the Child.* London: Routledge & Kegan Paul

Picone, Mary J. 1981. Aspects of Death Symbolism in Japanese Folk Religion. In P. G. O'Neill, ed., *Tradition and Modern Japan.* Tenterden, Kent: Paul Norbury

Pre-School Education in Japan. 1981. Ministry of Education, Science and Culture, Tokyo, Japan

Radcliffe-Brown, A. R. 1952. *Structure and Function.* London: Cohen and West

Raum, O. F. 1940. *Chaga Childhood.* Oxford University Press

Read, M. 1959. *Children of their Fathers: Growing up among the Ngoni of Nyasaland.* London: Methuen

Richards, Audrey I. 1970. Socialization and Contemporary British

BIBLIOGRAPHY

Anthropology. In Mayer, ed.
Richards, M. P. M., ed. 1974. *The Integration of a Child into a Social World*. Cambridge University Press
Richie, Donald. 1980. *Hadaka Matsuri* (Naked Festivals). In Hyoe Murakami & Donald Richie, eds., *A Hundred More Things Japanese*. Tokyo: Japan Cultural Institute
Riggs, Lynne E. 1977. *Ranjuku Jidai*. In 'The idioms of contemporary Japan'. *Japan Interpreter* 11: 541–9
Roberts, Joan I. & Sherrie K. Akinsanya. 1976. *Educational Patterns and Cultural Configurations: The Anthropology of Education*. New York: David McKay
Sato Katsuko. 1976. *Gendai Kazoku no Shitsuke* (Child-rearing in Modern Families). In Matsubara and Sato
Sakurai, Tokutaro. 1962. *Kōshudan Seiritsu Katei no Kenkyū (A Study on the Development of Kō Organization)*. Tokyo: Yoshikawa Kōbunkan
Sandberg, K. 1976. 'Some Contrasting Themes of Child-rearing in Japan and the United States' Unpublished manuscript, available from R. Hess, School of Education, Stanford University, Stanford, CA, 94305, USA
Seki, Keigo. 1962. *Nenrei Shudan* (Age Groups). In Omachi *et al.*, eds.
Shigaki, Irene S. 1983. 'Child care practices in Japan and the United States: how do they reflect cultural values in young children?' *Young Children* 38,4: 13–24
Shimahara, Nobuo K. 1979. *Adaptation and Education in Japan*. New York: Prager
Shiotsuki, Yaeko. 1970. *Kankonsōsai Nyūmon (An Introduction to Ceremonial)*. Tokyo: Kōbunsha
—— 1971. *Zukai Kankonsōsai (Illustrated Ceremonial)*. Tokyo: Kōbunsha
Siebold, Dr Ph.Fr.Von. 1841. *Manners and Customs of the Japanese*. London: John Murray
Silberman, Bernard S., ed. 1962. *Japanese Character and Culture: Selected Readings*. Tucson, Arizona: University of Arizona Press
Singer, Kurt. 1973. *Mirror, Sword and Jewel*, ed. R. Storry. London: Croom Helm
Singleton, J.1967. *Nichū: A Japanese School*. New York: Holt, Rinehart and Winston
Smith, Karen & Carmi Schooler. 1978. 'Women as mothers in Japan: the effects of social structure and culture on values and behaviour'. *Journal of Marriage and the Family*. 40,3: 613–20
Smith, Robert J. 1962. The Life Cycle. In Silberman, ed.
Smith, Thomas C. *et al.* 1977. *Nakahara*. Stanford, CA: Stanford University Press
Sofue, T. 1965. 'Childhood ceremonies in Japan: regional and local variations'. *Ethnology*. 4: 148–64
Statistical Handbook of Japan. 1984. Statistics Bureau, Prime Minister's Office
Stockwin, J. A. A. 1982. *Japan: Divided Politics in a Growth Economy*.

London: Weidenfield & Nicholson

Suzuki, Takao. 1973. *Kotoba to Bunka (Language and Culture)*. Tokyo: Iwanami Shoten

—— 1978. *Japanese and the Japanese* trans. Akira Miura. Tokyo: Kodansha International

Takeuchi, Toshimi. 1957. '*Kodomogumi ni tsuite*' ('The Children's Group'). *Minzokugaku Kenkyū (Japanese Journal of Ethnology)* 21,4: 61–7

Turner, Victor. 1963. *The Ritual Process*. London: Routledge & Kegan Paul

Vogel, Ezra. 1979. *Japan as Number One*. Cambridge, Mass: Harvard University Press

—— and Suzanne H. Vogel. 1961. 'Family security, personal immaturity and emotional health in a Japanese sample'. *Marriage and Family Living* 23: 161–6

Wakamori, Taro. 1973. Initiation Rites and Young Men's Organizations. In Dorson, R. M., *Studies in Japanese Folklore*. Port Washington, New York and London: Kennikat Press

Whiting, John W. M. and Irvin L. Child. 1953. *Child Training and Personality: A Cross-Cultural Study*. New Haven: Yale University Press

Williams, Thomas Rhys. 1972. *Introduction to Socialization: Human Culture Transmitted*. Saint Louis: C. V. Mosby

—— 1975. *Socialization and Communication in Primary Groups*. The Hague and Paris: Mouton

Wolfenstein, Martha. 1955. Fun Morality: An Analysis of Recent American Child-Training Literature. In Mead and Wolfenstein, eds.

Women and Education in Japan. 1980. Paper published by the Ministry of Education, Science and Culture (Japan): Social Education Bureau

Yamamoto Yoshiko. 1978. *The Namahage: A Festival in the Northeast of Japan*. Philadelphia: Institute for the Study of Human Issues (ISHI)

Yanagita, Kunio. 1957. *Japanese Manners and Customs in the Meiji Era*. Trans. and adapted by Charles Terry. Tokyo: Obunsha

Yōda, Akira. 1977. *Gendai no Hahaoya* (Mothers of Today). In Yoda & Ogawa, eds.

—— and Katsuyuki Ogawa, eds. 1977. '*Hahaoya*' ('Mothers'). *Gendai no Esupuri (The Spirit of Today)* No. 115. Tokyo: Shibundo

Yōji no Kokoroe (Understanding Early Childhood). *c*.1981. Manual published by Uzukyumeigan: Tokyo

Yokoe, Katsumi. 1970. Historical Trends in Home Discipline. In Hill and König

Index

Aberle, David F. 6
abortion rate 15
abunai 112–13, 157, 159, 160
age: 59, 64, 149, 167, 170–1; of
   rationality 104
aisatsu 73, 103
amae 18, 87; *amaeteru, amaekko* 87, 90
ancestral: memorials 53; tablets 14
anger 89, 180
annual events 40–1, 139–43, 169
anthropology: psychological 5; social 6
anticipation 23, 99, 154, 174
anxiety 21, 154
apology 73–4, 101, 111, 147, 165
aspirations of parents 91–5, 120–2
assembly 140, 169
atmosphere 97–9, 127, 150, 154, 164
authority 105, 147, 172

baby(ies): crying 90, 98; hotels 30, 48;
   identity of 81; in first year 47–8; in
   nursery 125–6, 129, 155, 167; sitters
   21, 154; talk 103
back-carrying 20, 54–5, 98
bathing 54, 80, 98–9, 102, 156; in
   company 54, 99
bed: time 19–21; wetting 43
Befu, Harumi 2, 105, 114, 173
belonging 115, 175
belongings 82, 129, 135, 137, 162, 165
Benedict, Ruth 6, 16, 102, 103
benevolence 56, 108, 163, 177; of
   teacher 65, 151; withdrawal of 110,
   159
Bernstein, Basil 173
birth 35
birthday 130, 169; first 37, 39; parties
   37, 65, 139, 167, 169; song 139
body: beautification of 11–12, 78, 173;
   boundaries of 82, 159; bodily contact
   98–9; control of 75, 139; bodily
   functions 155; positioning of 75;

stylised movements of 75; upper/
   lower distinction 76
books and pamphlets 2, 29, 48, 57, 99,
   131, 137
bowing 73, 75–6, 103, 134, 138, 140,
   163, 173
boundaries 82, 85, 157, 159, 160
boys' day 36, 40, 162
breast/bottle feeding 98, 154
bribes 105, 107, 164
Buddhism 42: ceremony 148; Japanese
   43; procession 42; temples 16, 62,
   126–7;

calendar 139
calligraphy 40–1, 66
celebrations and ceremonies 16, 34–43,
   45 n. 60, 58, 143, 181; adult 39;
   childhood 53; during pregnancy 34,
   39; first shrine visit 35, 39, 41, 162;
   'firsts' 36; graduation 169; life-cycle
   34; naming 35, 39; old age 40;
   opening & closing 140; purification
   39; seven-five-three 38–9, 41, 162;
   weaning 36, 39; *see also* birthday,
   boys' day, Buddhism, girls' day,
   sekku, Shinto
Chaga children 172
character: quality of 85–91, 122, 172
child(ren): as gift of gods 15–16; as
   treasure 16; born in Christian society
   16; identity of 74, 82, 115; interaction
   between 104; psychology, Western
   theories of 21; welfare services 29
Child Welfare Law 29, 121;
Christmas 41
churches 63, 126–7
classes 63–9, 128, 173, 181; for parents
   29; music 25, 67, 127; size of 123;
   violin 25, 127
classification 2, 7, 79, 81, 153, 174; of
   people 160–3

189